B. Traven

Government

ALLISON & BUSBY, London

This edition published in Great Britain 1980
by Allison & Busby, Limited,
6a Noel Street, London W1V 3RB

British Library Cataloguing in Publication Data

Traven, B.

  Government

  I. Title

  833'.9'1F   PT3919.T7W4

  ISBN 0-85031-356-2

  ISBN 0-85031-357-0 Pbk

Made and printed in Great Britain by
Billing & Sons Limited,
Guildford, London, Worcester

Government

1

The government was represented in the eastern district by don Casimiro Azcona. Like every other jefe político, don Casimiro thought first of his own interests. He served his country not for his country's good, but in order to profit at its expense. He worked better on those terms and, above all, he lived better. If a man can earn no more as a servant of the State than he can by running a snack bar, there is no reason whatever why he should aspire to devote his energies to his country's service.

After he had taken care of himself, he thought of his family. Then came his intimate friends. These friends had helped him obtain his post and now he had to humor them so that they would let him keep it, at least until one of them decided the moment had come to take it for himself.

Every member of his family to its remotest branches—nephews, cousins, brothers-in-law, uncles, brothers and their nephews, cousins, brothers-in-law, and sons—all were taken care of. They were given jobs as tax collectors, postmasters, chiefs of police, justices of the peace for as long as he himself could hold his. For this reason they were all on his side, whatever he might do. He might steal to his heart's content—provided always that when they in turn stole he did not order an inquiry into their conduct. Whatever they might do, lawfully or unlawfully, had to be right in his eyes.

This manner of administrating the public welfare began at the top with the president, don Porfirio, was carried on in the same fashion by his secretaries; it was taken up in turn by the generals, copied exactly by the governors of the various states, and handed on to the mayors of the smallest towns and villages. The whole system was called in newspapers and schoolbooks the intelligent and well-ordered organization of the Republic.

Since little if any ability was visible at the top, even less was looked for at the bottom. People were grateful to be allowed to live at all. And if a man was unexpectedly murdered because he had gotten heated over some administrative roguery or flagrant example of bribery and corruption, his neighbors and friends were only thankful that they themselves had escaped. The victim was buried and forgotten, and all he had by way of epitaph was "What did he want to burn his fingers for?"

2

Don Casimiro had a friend, don Gabriel Orduñez. This don Gabriel had been a cattle dealer but had gambled away almost all he possessed and drunk up what was left. Then he had opened a shop—until one day it was closed down by his creditors.

He was an old schoolfriend of don Casimiro's, and once when he was lamenting his troubles and the way he was dogged by bad luck, don Casimiro said, "I'll see if there's something I can do for you."

A few weeks later don Casimiro was on an inspection tour of the district and ran across don Gabriel again. Don Gabriel reminded him of his unfortunate situation, and as don Casimiro had a good heart and could not bear to see his friends suffer, he said, "I haven't much for you. Everything's gone. And they all sit as tight as ticks. But I've got a little Indian village—Bujvilum. A bad lot there. Won't behave themselves. Kick up against everything. We send soldiers to burn their huts down time after time—but can't catch one of them. They always clear out into the jungle and you can't get 'em there. When everything's burnt and their maize fields laid flat and the soldiers are gone, out they come and build up their village again as if nothing had happened. Then we leave them alone for a bit, but we can't get any taxes out of them. If you'd like to go there, I'll make you local secretary. You open a tienda, a little store. And I'll give you an exclusive permit to sell brandy. You have a lockup—a prison, in fact. I needn't say more. Well, there you are—if you want to go, the job's yours. I've nothing else for you at the moment."

Don Gabriel had a good revolver and he could shoot as straight as the next man. The Indians had no revolvers and could not buy any either; they had no money and, in any case, it was strictly forbidden to sell them revolvers or rifles, apart from muzzle-loaders for game. So don Gabriel accepted the post. He would have accepted the post of watching boiling cauldrons in hell if anyone had offered it to him. He was so down on his luck that he had no choice. It was getting on to twenty years since he had sought a way out in honest work. And a job in government is far and away the best. A man has only to keep his eyes open and pounce as soon as the prey shows its nose.

There was no reason for don Gabriel to be initiated into the details of his new post. There were no specific administrative regulations for that particular place, and even if there had been don Gabriel would not have needed to worry about them. He was a friend of the jefe político's; he had only to do as he saw fit and thought best. Every month he had to send the jefe a report giving the number of births, deaths, and cattle. If he had been compelled to shoot a few Indians he might put it down or not as he chose. In reporting such occurrences, he had only to be sure to state that they had taken place in self-defense and that the victims had publicly insulted the governor. No inquiry would follow—inquiries cost money. Besides, it was not to be imagined that a secretary, particularly when he was a friend of the political representative and had been recommended by him for the post, would falsify his reports.

3

Bujvilum was an independent Indian pueblo. It was inhabited by the Bachajontecs, a branch of the Tseltal tribe.

The Bachajontecs were very energetic Indians, industrious tillers of the soil and zealous raisers of cattle. Their cattle consisted of goats and sheep and large numbers of swine. The swine kept them in meat and lard, and from the sale of pigs to passing dealers they procured the money for things they could not themselves produce and had to buy in the larger towns of the district—machetes, axes, cotton goods, needles, powder, and buckshot.

Their wives made blankets, clothing, ponchos, and belts from the wool of the sheep. As these articles were well made and durable they were able to sell all that they did not need for their own use in the big market at Jovel. Their goods were always very much in demand and they could never produce enough to meet it.

The land of Bujvilum was very poor. That is why it had not been too greedily coveted by the Spanish colonizers. Later, when Mexico became independent, Mexicans tried to settle on it; but the Indians were a match for them and made their stay so unpleasant that the Ladinos—that is, those of them who remained alive—were always glad to curtail it. Outside their own district these Indians rarely did anyone any harm; that would only happen when they had sworn revenge and had good reason for it.

The Bachajontecs rebelled—against the government and individuals—only when they were not left in peace in their district. Passing travelers and dealers were safe as long as they spent no more than twenty-four hours in the place. But if they tried to lengthen their stay, the Indians became suspicious: they were afraid a pretext was being established for staying on as settlers. If the new arrival was still in the place on the second day, he was informed that his time was up and that he had better spend the night in the next place. If he did not take the hint, he was found murdered on the third morning, or at the latest, on the fourth. His goods or whatever else he had with him were left untouched in a room in the cabildo, where he had been sleeping.

The government, or, to be exact, the governor, was forever trying to bring Bujvilum under control—not because he was anxious for the well-being of these Indians, but because he could get no taxes from this industrious folk. It is no fun at all being a governor if no taxes come in.

Not that the Bachajontecs could altogether free themselves of taxes. If they took a pig or a few goats to another place to sell in the market, they had their market dues to pay. Besides these, the alcalde, the mayor of the town, took something a head on all animals sold—a peso for goats and as much as two pesos for a fully grown pig, a little less for partly grown animals.

When the Indians were on their way with their animals through smaller towns where they had no intention of selling, either because there were no buyers or because prices were bad, the alcaldes took a toll of twenty centavos for each animal driven through. It was very seldom they could avoid these places; they had to follow the roads that led from one town to another, owing to impassable bush and broken country which left them no other choice.

Even when it came to selling their handmade products, the Indians had to pay market dues; and if they had no money, then they had to surrender such a large part of the goods that the market dues were far more than paid for.

The Bachajontecs said nothing against these penalties. Every other Indian paid them. In any case, they could have said nothing, for they had no power outside their own territory. In their own pueblo, however, it was sometimes a different matter.

4

The governor would send twenty soldiers to accompany a newly appointed secretary to Bujvilum. All men and boys who had not fled in time into the jungle nearby were arrested and forced to build the cabildo. This was the official town hall. It was set off as government territory at a distance of a hundred paces or so from the nearest hut, or Indian jacal, of the village. For lack of other material the cabildo was built of sun-dried mud. It had one large room, which was the secretary's office; a second room was the schoolroom, a third was the secretary's living quarters, and a fourth room was the prison.

The prison was very important—as everywhere on earth. Everywhere the building of a prison is the first step in the organization of a civilized state.

As soon as the cabildo was completed it was inaugurated. The new secretary provided a few fireworks, which were set off at night with great jubilation. He further provided a keg of brandy to put the Indians in a good frame of mind. He made a speech in which much was said of la patria and amor por la patria and much was promised for the honradez—the uprightness and justice—which would mark his administration.

Then the jefe of the Indians was called upon to speak. In the name of his people the chief promised to support the secretary with all his power in every just undertaking and to promote with zeal the well-being of the place and of all its native population.

A message was sent to the governor, announcing the excellent understanding between the Indians and the representative of the government, namely, the secretary. The governor replied with a message of thanks and the promise of his protection.

The Indians who had fled into the jungle with their families came back with their cattle and set about cultivating their fields. Peace and harmony were the order of the day.

Then the place was connected by telephone with the nearest municipalidad, a county seat where there was a garrison. As soon as the telephone wires were laid, a small commission dispatched by the Department of Health arrived and all the Indians were vaccinated and given a few doses of quinine.

Two weeks after they had arrived the soldiers were lined up in front of the cabildo, called to attention, and then, shouldering their rifles, they marched back to their garrison.

5

The secretary could not live and support a family on his paltry salary, and the government did not expect him to. He was, after all, the secretary of a place inhabited by active and industrious Indians.

No one expected a governor, a chief of police, a mayor, or a tax collector to live on his pay; nor did the jefe político imagine for a moment that he had to live on his.

So it was also a matter for the secretary to consider how he was to arrive at a decent income for himself. The jefe político expected a good share of it, just as a chief of police looked to the police under his command for a share of their pickings, in order to feel justified in continuing to employ them. How they came by their pickings was no affair of his. They were all born with heads on their shoulders, and he had given them each a good revolver and invested them with ample authority.

So the secretary labored and labored to increase his income and to live up to the hopes of the jefe político, who wrote to him every fortnight, intimating that he required a further consideration and that it was high time it arrived.

It depended entirely on the manner in which the secretary labored whether six or eight or even eighteen months passed by in peace. But ultimately one morning he found his best cow slaughtered, a week later his last one. Then his horse was found with a deep gash in the leg from a machete. Then the telephone wire was cut. He set out to find the place. At a spot where the bush was densest he found a fine new red woolen belt. As he bent down to pick it up, a machete whizzed by, an inch from his head. After that he did not dare leave the cabildo. And he could not telephone. One evening he stood smoking a cigarette beneath the portico of the cabildo contemplating the weather. As he turned to go in again and was just about to shut the door, there was a report. A great lump of shot pierced his hat and dug its way into the door.

Next morning he packed up, put his family on horseback, and cleared out, never to return. The village was like a home of the dead, but he knew that a hundred eyes watched his departure through the bamboo poles of the jacales.

If he did not go, then two or three or ten days later he was a dead man.

A few weeks afterward the soldiers came. The jefe político had had no report for three months, so he had sent soldiers to investigate.

The soldiers searched the huts. They found not a soul in them. Even the pots and pans were gone. They burned all the huts to the ground. The cabildo, with the ruins of the prison, was left standing.

Their rations gone, and with not even a dried-up tortilla to be found, the soldiers marched off again.

After a few months the governor decided once more to bring

the place to heel and tax it in the name of the government.
The jefe político had a friend for whom a job had to be found
because he was forever pursued by bad luck and harassed for
money. So the soldiers arrived once more, bringing the new
secretary and his family with them. But there was nowhere for
the new secretary to live. The cabildo had been burned down
and wiry grass and vigorous scrub covered the place where it
had once stood.

The village had been built up again. The maize was green in
the fields. But there was not a soul in the village, not a goat or
a sheep, not a pot or a pan in the jacales.

The jungle was dense, dark, and menacing. There were no
paths, and it was full of marshes, tigers, snakes, and mosqui-
toes. The sergeant in charge of the soldiers was an Indian. He
knew what jungle and bush were like. He had no desire to go
catching Indians in the jungle to build the cabildo.

Word was sent to the jefe político. The maize fields were
green and promising. Taxes beckoned. The jefe político, who
was in chronic need of money and who had for that reason
made a friend of his the new secretary, could not afford to
leave the village in peace. He needed money, and it was there
to be got if the secretary knew how to go about it.

He sent a message to the secretary of another independent
Indian community, situated nearer the garrison, telling the
secretary to have the Indian jefe of the village send twenty of
his people to rebuild the cabildo, without pay, without even
their rations—for the new secretary had to have his office and
somewhere to live and the telephone and a prison.

The cabildo was built. The Indians reappeared out of the
jungle. Fireworks were set off and speeches made about la
patria. The soldiers slung their rifles across their shoulders and
marched off.

Ten or twelve months wents by, and then one day a machete
missed the head of the new secretary by a hair's breadth.

The village was once more burned to the ground. Then wiry grass flourished again on the spot where the new cabildo with its prison had stood, and then the soldiers arrived once more.

So it had gone on over the years. It came and went like the seasons. There might be revolutions; there might be military uprisings; the presidents might be murdered or go to Europe for their health in fear of being murdered—but in Bujvilum nothing changed.

And all this came and went not because these independent Indians were savages and rebels and murderers, or because they could not adapt themselves to the organization of a justly administered state, but because governors and jefe políticos and other officials were in chronic need of money; because they gambled and whored; because they tolerated and carried in their train a mob of parasites, called friends and relations; because they had three times more women than they could feed, clothe, and hang with jewels.

6

It sometimes happened that Bujvilum was without a secretary for five years at a stretch or longer. It owed this good fortune to the fact that the place was forgotten; and it was most likely to be forgotten when the higher powers were at loggerheads.

A new governor had been elected. He maintained that he had a majority; but his defeated opponent maintained and proved that the returns had been faked, and that if they had not been faked he would have been the elected governor. So he took office and established his government in another town in the state and hastened to put all his friends into jobs so as to have their support. The elected governor did the same in order to follow up his success; for the best way to follow up a success is to have as many followers as possible.

And now since these two new governors were irreconcilably

at odds, it was the patriotic duty of the outgoing governor to remain in office also.

The federal government, which could not keep out of this imbroglio in case it lost control of the state, appointed a provisional governor who likewise assumed office.

Now, in Mexico there were always two governments, the civil and the military. Each state had two regents, the governor and the jefe de las operaciones militares. This jefe was the commanding officer of the federal troops in the garrisons throughout the state. As this general had been made responsible for the preservation of peace in the state, he held it his duty to set up a provisional governor on his own account, because he did not feel able to give the governor provisionally set up by the federal government his confidence and with it his military support.

So it came about that there were five governors exercising authority over the state at the same time, all warring against one another since none would give way. Each had a lengthy train of friends and relations and each was determined to make the fullest use of his time in office in order to set himself up for the rest of his days. All maintained emphatically that they were inspired by the purest and most unselfish love of their country.

Similar battles were frequently waged among the jefe políticos. And these were the periods when the Indians of independent villages in the remoter regions lived in peace. Dogs experience the same thing: when the bacon is being fought for, the bones are overlooked, but when possession of the bacon has been thrashed out then the bones become important.

During the dictatorship of don Porfirio the bacon was settled. He had it, and he divided it at leisure among his fat retainers, all the relations and friends who sucked his blood. Those who were too remote from him to be of any danger or use did without the bacon and had to be content with the bones. And there were bones to be picked far and wide in this vast country. Every man who worked, every man who produced anything was a bone from which it was the duty of every jack-in-office to extract the marrow. Whether you looked at it from inside or out you got the same impression—that to have any office meant nothing but the opportunity to get rich.

There was no fear of being hauled over the coals unless the holder of an office was suspected of being unfriendly to the dictatorship, or, worse, of babbling about democracy, universal suffrage, and the ineligibility of a president for re-election. That was the one crime of which an official could be guilty. He himself had supreme jurisdiction over any other crimes and corruptions he might commit and practice. Where there is a dictator at the top of the ladder, you find nothing but dictators on every other rung. The only difference is that some are higher up and others lower down.

Those who occupied the lower rungs were the big businessmen, the manufacturers, the large landholders, the mining companies, the owners of plantations, and the proprietors of large farms—the finqueros.

7

Don Gabriel was no innocent infant at the breast. He knew how it fared with secretaries in the independent Indian pueblos. Hundreds of instances were known to him, as they were to everybody in the state.

But he also knew, from hundreds of examples, what a secretary of these Indian communities could make if he was up to his job. And that was what decided him to accept the post with alacrity as soon as it was offered him. Like all secretaries before him, he decided to crack the bone as fast as he could and then to make himself scarce with equal speed before the Indians were stung to frenzy.

The Indians were far from being ill disposed. They were not

warlike. They were tillers of the soil, who are everywhere of a peaceable disposition as long as they are left to go their own way. They have no other desire but to cultivate their fields in peace, to support their families, to rear their children, and to enjoy a quiet old age. Agriculture rules out the warlike spirit. Fields and herds go to ruin if men have to be out on the war-path; and if on a foray they lay waste the fields of their neigh-bors, these neighbors are then compelled to support themselves by overrunning the fields of the aggressors in turn. Agriculture is no nursery of adventure. The adventurous and warlike spirit arises only when his own land no longer supports the agri-culturalist.

Don Gabriel knew Bujvilum and he knew the Bachajontecs. He had often dealt with them as a cattle buyer and had always found them easy to get on with in the way of business. Know-ing their friendly disposition he had no fear of going among them as secretary.

8

It was three years since the Bachajontecs had had a secretary. Their last one had died in his bed, of fever or a cramp in the stomach. In any case, he had departed this life by a natural death. It is true that he had not brought matters to such a pass as to have a shower of lead about his ears as a warning to remove himself and his family before worse happened. His wife had stayed on with his children for a few months and carried on the official duties of her deceased husband. Then when her tienda was sold out she had returned to her home at Shcuchuitz.

After this the place had been without a secretary because the jefe político could not find a suitable man who was willing to go, and those who did want to go spoke not a word of Tseltal.

Don Gabriel took a few soldiers with him, as every secretary always did; in his case it was not for protection, but because they were the only document the Indians could read. The soldiers were the announcement of don Gabriel's formal appointment as the new secretary who was to represent the government in Bujvilum.

As always when soldiers approached the place, the Indians vanished into the jungle; but some of them soon emerged when they saw that the soldiers had stacked their arms in front of the cabildo and lain down to sleep without having entered the village area to search the huts.

As soon as the advance party of Indians returned to the village, the soldiers bought poultry and eggs from them and paid, in hard cash. Then, their purchases completed, they returned to their camp and set about cooking their evening meal.

Next morning don Gabriel hoisted the national flag on a high pole in front of the cabildo. The soldiers stood at attention and the trumpeter sounded the flag salute. Then the soldiers marched away.

At night don Gabriel hauled down the flag and set off a few fireworks. He did not dole out brandy, as the few men who had come back to the village remained in their huts. That same night some of them went into the jungle to tell the people that the soldiers had gone and that there were only the new secretary and his wife in the cabildo. In the morning smoke ascended peacefully from the hearths of all the jacales.

One by one the men approached the cabildo. The jefe of the village introduced himself and his delegates—his elected councilors—to the new secretary.

When the men saw that don Gabriel had meanwhile opened his tienda they began making purchases at once. A little later the women and children came too and bought salt, needles and thread, candy, tobacco, and coffee.

The cabildo, which was constructed of thin stakes daubed with mud and roofed with palm leaves, was in a wretched condition. Without don Gabriel's having to say a word, the men came at midday and began repairing the building, and particularly the flimsy roof. They also replaced the half-rotted door of the prison with a strong new wooden one with a grating.

"That'll stop murderers and criminals breaking out," said the jefe as his men brought the new door along.

Don Gabriel gave each man who had worked on the cabildo a copita—a nip of brandy. The jefe refused. He never touched aguardiente, he said.

That night don Gabriel said to his wife, "I say, the viejo, the casique, doesn't drink. I don't like the looks of it."

"He'll drink quick enough," his wife replied reassuringly. "He'd be the first I've known who didn't. Try him when he's alone with you."

9

Don Gabriel could never grow rich on the proceeds of the store. For one thing, the store was not large. It took up just a corner of their room, where an opening had been made in the mud wall. This opening was closed by a stout wooden shutter; at the bottom of it were two loops of bast which were passed over pegs in the wall, so that it could be either let down or held up. When it was let down the opening in the wall was like an open window. The board had two hinged supports on which it rested, and in this way the shutter became the counter when the store was open. If anybody wanted to buy anything he stood outside at the opening and waited patiently, without calling or rapping, until don Gabriel or his wife chanced to notice that there was a customer in the shop—as one might say elsewhere. When the shutter was up, the store was closed.

For another thing, the store was not well stocked. No one had allowed don Gabriel a centavo's worth of merchandise on credit, not even when he said he had been appointed a secretary; and so he had been limited in the purchase of his stock by the ready money in his possession—and this was very little.

The few pesos he had been able to borrow from friends and relations of his wife had gone for household and traveling expenses.

The one thing he had got on credit was a keg of aguardiente —the low-quality brandy sold to the Indians of Mexico—and that at an outrageous price against his promissory note, payable on the last day of the second month without further notice or warning. Don Gabriel's wife had had to sign as surety. The brandy distiller, however, had agreed to let him have aguardiente at the usual wholesale price in the future on a month's credit, if he met the first bill on the date when it fell due.

Aguardiente cannot be sold on credit to Indians in Mexico. In small places with a purely Indian population no brandy can be sold at all. But don Gabriel had been given a special license for the sale of brandy by the jefe político, who could make and unmake laws according to his own discretion in his own district, just as the governor could in the state he governed.

Laws for the common good are all very well. But there must always be officials to see that the laws are honored, and these officials who have power and authority to see that the laws are honored must be strong enough in their own sphere to go beyond or to alter or to tighten up the laws just as they see fit. Otherwise there would be no sense in a dictatorship and you might just as well have a democracy. There has got to be some difference, after all. And the dictator who is at the top could not maintain his dictatorship very long without good friends who in their turn exercised power and authority under him.

Don Gabriel sold four small glasses of brandy on the second day, one on the third, none on the fourth, two on the fifth, and on the sixth, a Sunday, none.

That evening don Gabriel remarked to his wife, "If I don't give credit I won't sell the keg in four months, and how I can pay the bill in six weeks is more than I know."

"Of course you'll have to give credit, tonto, you idiot," his wife replied. "The fellows'll pay up all right when they sell some pigs or maize or wool."

Don Gabriel's receipts for the week from the sale of goods from the store amounted to two pesos thirty centavos. True, there was no fear of starving. The people in the village were not unfriendly. One day a man brought him a hen as a present, another day he was given a kid, the day afterward he got a sackful of maize, and the day after that a heavy cluster of golden bananas. And the Indian jefe gave him a plot from the communal land and also sent some boys to put it in order for him.

But what don Gabriel wanted was money. You cannot make your pile out of maize, poultry, and eggs unless you deal in them wholesale and have a ready market.

What was the good of having power in the place if it was not put to use? When you have power you must use it—and use it quickly before you lose it.

10

Two Syrian peddlers passed through the village. They had a variety of useful articles to sell and a lot of trash besides—matches, printed cotton, cloth, buttons, many-colored combs of celluloid, hairpins, needles, white shirt material, knives, spoons, brightly enameled cups, percussion caps, glass beads, gawdy rings and earrings, bicarbonate of soda, quinine, pictures of saints with looking glasses on the back, gay silk scarves, thread.

The Indian is very much like the rest of us. The women love bright ribbons and gawdy necklaces and gleaming earrings; and like all other women on earth they pass very easily from the important things required for the household and for clothing to the purchase of innumerable other things which give them pleasure or distinguish them from other women and attract the attention of their husbands or their lovers. Here too, as everywhere else, the husband is induced to let his wife buy what she likes by the persuasion of laughter and cajolery or of tears and cross looks. And the man too, as elsewhere, buys all sorts of things which are of little use, merely because he thinks they will give his wife pleasure or open the heart of a girl to his courtship.

The traders who go from one Indian village to another with their pack mules know from long experience how best to do business. They know how to get rid of what they have brought with them, whether it is what the Indians need or not. It matters no more to them than it does to other merchants whether the articles they offer for sale are useful or are trash; all that matters to them is that they are salable and bring a good profit.

Traveling peddlers, when they arrived at a place to sell their goods, went first to the alcalde and introduced themselves. It was a polite formality. The alcalde sometimes asked to see their license and tax receipts and informed them that they could not sell brandy.

The two Syrians went first to don Gabriel. True, he was not the alcalde. The head man of the village was the casique, the jefe elected by the Indians. But the dealers regarded the secretary as the real man in authority, and don Gabriel would have taken it very much amiss if they had not.

When they saw that he sold brandy, they first had a drink and stood him to one too, to increase the outlay. Then they asked whether they might spend the night in the cabildo and have their meal with him. That again gave him a chance to make something.

The two traders paid up to the hilt in federal taxes, they paid state taxes, and they paid rates in the municipalidad where they lived. Besides all this they paid for a special license as peddlers.

Don Gabriel did not examine their licenses and their receipts for taxes paid. It was of no interest to him what others made on them. As soon as the copitas were downed he came straight to the point.

"There is a special tax for the village here, one peso a day for each trader."

"But," objected one of the Syrians, "we have paid already for a license from the municipalidad in Jovel."

"What you fellows pay in Jovel is no concern of mine," he snapped. "You come here to do business and so you've got to pay a tax. If you don't pay, you get no permission from me to display your goods or to go to people's homes, and you leave the place within an hour."

"But that is an injustice," said the other of the two.

To this don Gabriel replied: "I am secretary here and I know whether there is a tax to be paid in this place or not."

The Syrians paid.

"There is no need to write you a receipt," he said, as he took the money. "I am here on the spot and no one in another place will want a receipt for taxes paid here."

Thus they had no proof if they should wish to bring a complaint. They would not in any case have got very far with a complaint even if they had had a receipt to show. Dictatorships and military regimes don't hold with complaints and the right to complain; and those who open their mouths get shot as disturbers of the peace and resisters of authority.

Don Gabriel was not through with them yet, however. When you have hooked a fish you must keep a firm hold on the line.

"I get no pay to speak of here," he said. "My pay consists in the right to run a store and sell brandy. You come along to sell the same things that I have in my tienda, and if you sell them it means that I can't sell them. You must each pay me an additional peso a day in consideration of your competition and as some compensation for the harm you do me."

The two traders paid this too.

It is the case everywhere that when a half-cent tax is put on a package of cigarettes, the retailer sells the package not for half a cent more but for five cents more—"by way of adjustment," as he says. He justifies the increased price by the new tax.

Here these traders at once added 50 per cent to all their prices. The Indians, who had no alternative, paid it. Don Gabriel, who as secretary was supposed to protect the Indians against extortion and robbery, could say nothing against these exorbitant prices because it was by his authority that the traders were permitted to do business in the place.

11

Don Gabriel was kind and obliging. When he saw that many of the Indians wanted to buy material for shirts and other necessities but had no money, he offered them credit—quite of his own accord. His only regret was in not having more cash on hand to lend out, though the sum he had just collected from the traders was a help.

"You want a loan of three pesos, Hipolito?" he asked.

"Yes, don Gabriel. I have no shirt and my wife says we must have a few yards of cloth."

"You can have three pesos and welcome," said don Gabriel. "Who will stand surety for you?"

"My brother Eleoso."

"Bring him to me."

"I'm here," said Eleoso.

"You'll stand surety for Hipolito?"

"Of course. He's my brother."

"When are you going to sell those two pigs of yours, Hipolito?" asked don Gabriel.

"In five weeks, don Gabriel. I've spoken to don Roberto about it already. He is the dealer who always comes here to buy pigs and goats."

"Then in five weeks, you'll give me five pesos. Is that so, Hipolito?"

"Certainly, I'll give you the five pesos then," said Hipolito.

"You'll answer for the five pesos in five weeks, Eleoso?" said don Gabriel. "And a peso for every week over?"

"Certainly, I'll answer for my brother," said Eleoso.

"Good. Then here are your three pesos," said don Gabriel, giving the money to Hipolito, who at once bought material for shirts.

Don Gabriel lent out all the ready money he had in the house to the Indians who wanted to buy from the traders; and as the people got the money so easily, they spent it to the last centavo.

12

A few weeks later cattle dealers arrived on the scene.

"So you want to buy up animals?" don Gabriel asked when they had drunk a few rounds.

"Yes, we come regularly," they said. "We make good purchases here."

"You know about the local taxes?" asked don Gabriel.

"We pay taxes where our homes are as well as the local rate for our slaughterhouses."

"It doesn't concern me what you pay elsewhere," said don Gabriel. "For every pig you buy here, you have a peso and a half to pay, for each sheep a peso, and for each goat eighty centavos. Unless you pay it I cannot give you permission to do business, nor can I give the villagers permission to sell to you."

Now the dealers had come a long way and they wanted to keep the business they had in the place, but in order to realize their profit they had to offer the Indians much less for their animals than they had expected, so as to make up for the tax they had to pay.

The Indians refused to sell at the prices offered and said they would drive their animals to Jovel, where they would be sure to get the old prices for them. The dealers became angry and refused in turn to buy. They said they would have a look around in other places.

If they did not buy, don Gabriel would not pocket his tax; but this time, too, he did not let the fish he had hooked escape him. He summoned the jefe of the Indians.

Whenever don Gabriel wanted to carry his point with the Indians and was afraid it might lead to vehement opposition and long-winded explanations, he always allowed the decision to rest with their own chief, to whom they had themselves given authority. That way he remained merely the modest secretary who recognized the authority of the head man of the place; for the actual ruler of the community was always an Indian, a member of the tribe which for hundreds of years had been settled there. This local chief was elected by the Indians each year from among the reputable and competent men of the tribe. The secretary was no more than the representative of the government, who, because the Indians could not read and write, acted as a link between the government and the community. He had no right to dispose of any matter or to make regulations without the consent of the Indian jefe.

So the law ordained. The law was made not out of love of the Indians and not out of consideration for their natural rights, but because it was the only means by which the government could live in peace with the independent Indians. Military expeditions to try to keep them otherwise under government control were costly. And even when an expedition went out and soldiers succeeded in destroying whole Indian villages, the Indians who were driven from their homes formed bands and went about robbing and murdering and plundering among the farms and villages of the Mexican population, burning haciendas and whole settlements to the ground, slaughtering cattle, burning crops, destroying telegraph wires and bridges, stealing horses and mules from the prairies, and causing so much damage that the government hastened to make peace with them.

The Indians had no liking for wandering about in bands. They preferred to live quietly in their villages, surrounded by their families, cultivating their fields and rearing their animals. Not only the government but the whole country benefited when the Indians were left in peace.

But even though the law left the Indians complete self-government in all places where the population was exclusively Indian, the law was still subject to the interpretation the secretaries chose to give to it and to the manner in which they applied it. It is always the interpretation of laws and what follows from it that does the mischief.

13

Don Gabriel could carry out what he intended only with the help of the Indian jefe. "Look here, Narciso," don Gabriel said to him, "this is how it stands. These nine men"—and he named them all—"have all borrowed money from me, one more, another less. They all gave me security when they borrowed the money. The money is now due. They promised to pay me back as soon as they sold pigs or sheep. Now the dealers are here and the men won't sell, because the price doesn't suit them. But that is no fault of mine."

"No, certainly not," said the jefe.

"They want to sell their animals at Jovel market," don Gabriel went on, "because they think they'll get a better price. But if so many animals are all driven at once to market, the prices will be lower than they're offered here. Of course, that does not matter to me. But there's this in it, don Narciso"—he now addressed the Indian as "don" to show that he put him on an equality with a Ladino—"you see, if the people sell their animals in Jovel, they'll spend their money there on drink, and then how will they pay me back the money which is due and for which others have stood surety?"

Narciso at once had all the men whom don Gabriel had

named brought before him. He asked each what he owed don Gabriel, counting the interest for which he had given security.

Don Gabriel had his book in his hand and he checked the amounts which each debtor carried in his head. Not one tried to give a wrong figure. They would never do that, for their word was their bond and they stood by it.

"Then you promised," asked Narciso, "and produced sureties, that as soon as dealers came to the village you would sell pigs or whatever else you had, so as to pay back to don Gabriel the money you had borrowed?"

The men admitted it, but said that the prices the dealers offered were much lower than they had always paid before.

"I can't help that," said Narciso.

He turned to one of the dealers. "Why are prices so low all of a sudden? For years they have never been so low."

The dealer was about to answer when, looking around, he saw don Gabriel's eye fixed upon him. He had been ready to say that he had such a heavy tax to pay per head on all animals he bought here that he had to give less in order to make any profit at all when selling to the butchers.

But don Gabriel did not let him speak. "Rates and taxes are so high now," he said, "that the dealers can't pay the old prices."

The dealer fell in with this at once. He saw that it would never do to cross up the secretary if he wanted to do business there. A secretary could find a hundred ways of putting difficulties in a dealer's path and could make it impossible for him to buy so much as a skin as long as he remained secretary of the place. What could the dealer do if the secretary said that the animals he had bought in another village had a contagious disease and had to be destroyed at once to prevent the infection from spreading? The animals would be killed and burned. How or to whom could the dealer prove that they were not sick at all? Don Gabriel would not have been the first to resort to such measures if a dealer or anyone else who came to the place disputed his word and authority as secretary.

Narciso, the chief of the Indians, could only judge by what he saw and heard. The men had contracted debts with don Gabriel and had promised to pay the debts as soon as a dealer arrived to whom they could sell their animals. He recognized that don Gabriel's claim was just and that no one disputed it. So his verdict was that all the men who owed don Gabriel money had to sell animals to the dealers at the best prices they felt they could offer. The other men might do as they liked.

All the men of the village had meanwhile gathered in the open space in front of the cabildo, for the proceedings had taken a leisurely course and lasted some hours. The men, even the debtors, agreed that their chief had settled the dispute justly. As none of them knew, or could have known, anything about the bargain don Gabriel had made with the dealers, they recognized the justice of the jefe's verdict. And as it was not the secretary, whom none of them trusted, but their own chief who had given the verdict, they willingly submitted to it and the dealers got even more animals than they had hoped for.

"Now you see how foolish you were to have made a fuss over the few pesos I take off you," don Gabriel said to the dealers that evening. "If I hadn't been behind you, you wouldn't have seen so much as the tail of a lousy goat. And look at you now—where else could you have made such a haul as you have here? You've no occasion whatever to pull a long face over the few miserable pesos that find their way into my pocket."

His job, which at first had looked like a very lean one, now appeared to have possibilities.

2

 The few pesos don Gabriel had handed out had come back to him, bringing their sheaves with them; and he was now in a position to extend his operations.

One of his duties was the opening of a school. It was one of the many sidelines of his office, a sideline he could easily find time for, since his chief function, properly speaking, was merely to be on the spot.

He had never been a schoolteacher. He could read and write and do simple arithmetic, and with that his qualifications to teach began and ended. But the dictatorship set little store by the education of the common people. As soon as they had any education their wants increased and they became discontented with the life which God, with the help of the Church and the State, had made for them and in which it was His desire they should remain.

But then, tourists and journalists came into the country from abroad, and people came who had money and wanted to invest it to advantage in a country where competition was less severe and exacting than in their own. The dictator wanted to see the country opened up and taking its place in the ranks of highly civilized nations. The dictator of a highly civilized nation is looked up to and his place in history is more secure than that of a dictator who rules a horde of savages. The Mexicans, in the dictator's opinion, were not capable of opening up the country themselves. They did not know how to work and, besides, they did not want to work.

He himself, though a Mexican, was an exception. That was why he allowed himself to be elected time after time by those to whom he gave the right to elect him and who in return were rewarded with offices and jobs. The farce of election was kept up in order to demonstrate to civilized countries that this was a constitutionally conducted republic, where foreign capital could safely be invested and concessions safely taken up by the American banks and mining companies.

The dictator thought himself the best Mexican alive and the only Mexican whose life was of consequence.

When the elections came around he gave solemn audience to his following and allowed himself to be implored to run again. He then turned a deaf ear like some millionaire's flunky who is above taking a tip but is grievously disappointed if it is not placed in the open palm he holds behind his back. Finally, when his followers begged him on their knees to consent, the dictator declared that it had not been his intention to run again. He had taken an oath not to be a candidate for election, "but since, caballeros, you insist upon it, I will sacrifice my personal inclinations once again for the sake of the people of Mexico."

This was reported in all the American newspapers and the world knew that Mexico was not governed by a despotic dictator. It was an up-to-date and civilized republic with a highly developed constitutional system.

The dictator sacrificed himself for his people in this manner eight times in succession, until a protracted and bloody revolution threw him out of the saddle. The ungrateful Mexican people allowed their great statesman to die in exile in a foreign land, embittered and sorrowing.

One of the most important tasks the dictator set himself was to cook up statistics for the benefit of the world at large. If he had neglected to do this, the world would never have known what a great statesman he was and what a debt of gratitude the Mexican people owed him for sacrificing himself again and again, bearing the heavy burden of dictatorship and wearing the president's crown of thorns, in order to be the first and foremost of the servants of his beloved people.

Countless hordes of bandits, composed of Indians whose land had been taken from them and given to the big landowners, American companies, and members of the aristocratic clique, roamed the country and were joined by peons who had fled from the tyranny of the landowners. These hordes were put down by the dictator's iron hand—insofar, at least, that no newspaper might make any allusion to them on pain of confiscation.

But the dictator did not want merely to show the iron hand of a great statesman who guaranteed peace and security within his country's borders; he wanted also to have the reputation in civilized countries of being the man who educated the people of Mexico. This fame he achieved by means of statistics showing the number of schools he had opened in the country, in order to provide the children of Indians and peons and, indeed, of all the working people with up-to-date instruction.

A country which has many schools stands high in the scale of civilized nations, and there is nothing like it for attracting foreign capital and investments. The schools in the large towns were quite as good as the schools in the United States. They had to be, for the tourists, bankers, and journalists who came to these towns were invited to inspect them.

These gentry did not, however, go to the remote Indian villages. Instead they were given statistics on all the village schools which the dictator had established, and with this the foreign visitors were content. They quailed at the thought of arduous journeys into the interior of the country, and saw all they wanted of village schools from the beautifully made models of rural schoolhouses which were exhibited in the Department of Education.

The escuela rural, the village school at Bujvilum, of which don Gabriel was the teacher, was one of the schools established by the great statesman-educator of the Mexican people, and it was glorified in the returns as a school for Indians with one hundred and twenty scholars.

This village school at Bujvilum was conducted in very much the same way as all other village schools of the Republic. It had in fact one hundred and twenty scholars of the male sex. The statistics did not lie.

2

"How many boys are there in Bujvilum and the outlying places belonging to it?" don Gabriel asked Narciso, the chief.

"I will have them counted," said Narciso.

He brought the answer a few days later. "A hundred and twenty, or perhaps a few more."

"They must all come here to school," don Gabriel announced.

The jefe gave the order.

Next Monday morning about thirty boys, most of them naked, came to school. Don Gabriel wrote down all their names. If any of them did not know their last names, because they had never heard them, he gave them names of his own selection.

On Tuesday there were again thirty; half of them were new ones who had not come on Monday. The others were absent because don Gabriel, not knowing what to do with his pupils, had beaten three of them for the sake of doing something and to show them what school was for. Some of the fathers, on hearing of this, had not been pleased and so had forbidden their children to go to school again. They did not see why the secretary should beat the boys merely because they horsed around in the open space in front of the cabildo.

Don Gabriel again beat a few of the boys—after all, he was the schoolteacher. Next day half the boys were again absent. They preferred working in the fields with their fathers to going to school to be beaten. But a dozen new ones came who had not been there either on Monday or Tuesday. And in the course of two weeks each of the hundred and twenty had been to school at least once.

Don Gabriel sent his report in to the government, giving a list of one hundred and twenty scholars. The school appeared in the statistics and made a very good impression there.

Now that don Gabriel had scholars every day, he had to teach them. The boys arrived at six in the morning as they had been instructed to do—or, to be accurate, at sunrise, for neither don Gabriel nor anyone else in the place had a clock. Don Gabriel himself had not yet left his bed. Only his wife was up and about.

At about half-past seven he had his coffee. Then at last he went to the door and called out, "Are you all there, muchachos?"

"Yes, señor Profesor, we are all here," the boys shouted back.

"I am coming in a moment. Don't make so much noise," don Gabriel called, and for a time the boys sat on the grass as still as mice.

But while don Gabriel was lounging about indoors and quarreling with his wife because he had no idea what to do next, the boys went back to running around and chasing each other. In about an hour don Gabriel appeared at the door again, in a very bad temper after one of the usual arguments with his wife, and called out, "Didn't I tell you to keep quiet, you vermin?"

Grabbing one of the boys, he gave him a clout on the ear. The boy set up a howl and cried out, "I'll tell my father you hit me." Then he ran off to his home and did not return that day.

After a while the boys began horsing around again, trying to see which of them could stand on his head the longest. Don Gabriel was now having his breakfast.

"And now these filthy beans are only half cooked," he said to his wife. "Damn it all, if you can't cook, what did you marry for? Your mother's another fine customer—has nothing and knows nothing and squanders all she gets from don Manuel. He has all my sympathy for being your father. The tortillas are cold and taste like straw. Some life this. What have I done to be mixed up with a family like yours? Your brother Sixto is nothing but a common thief. There's not a girl safe from him either. Strike me blind if they don't stand him up against a wall one of these days and shoot the bum."

"Leave my family out of it, do you hear?" his wife screamed back at him. "Your family's known far and wide. They've nothing in front and still less behind, and more debts than lice. I only wish I'd listened to a good mother's advice. She warned me against you from the first. God knows how right she was. Your mother isn't fit to sweep the floor for her. I'd better have hanged myself than had anything to do with a cur like you." With this she sat down in a corner and began to howl.

Don Gabriel slapped the tortilla he had in his hand down on his plate in a rage and, rushing out the door, snatched up a stick and hurled it with all his might into the mob of romping boys.

"Haven't I told you a hundred times not to shout like that? I'll flog every one of you, and quick too!"

Some of the boys ran off to the village crying out as they went, but the more forbearing stayed where they were and squatted on the grass without making a sound, like intimidated earthworms who have forgotten which hole they crawled out

of and can hope for nothing better than to be found by a
blackbird and put out of their misery.

3

It was now ten o'clock. Don Gabriel spent some time in his
office, just to see if anything might have turned up. Nothing
did.

Nothing could possibly have turned up, for his official business at Bujvilum moved very slowly. He looked around to see
if there was anything he could conceivably do, since after all,
he was the secretary of the place. But look around as he might
there was nothing to call for governmental activity.

Everything was exactly as he had left it the night before.
There were a few papers and letters on the table, others were
spiked on some nails in the mud wall. He shuffled the letters
and printed orders and regulations about. He had already
looked over every leaflet and scrap of paper a hundred times
without bothering his head for a moment over a single thing
they said. In his position he ought to have had a clerk, but he
did not; nor would he have known how to employ one, for
there was nothing that called for clerical activities. He could
only have given him the papers to copy out in order to keep
him occupied.

When he had shuffled the papers several times he placed
them as they had been before, smoothed them out and aligned
them accurately with the corner of the table; then he gave
them a pat to ensure that they would consent to remain where
he had put them.

After this, he took up the ink bottle, shook it, uncorked it,
smelled it, shook it again, corked it up, and put it back in its
place. Then he picked up his pen and examined the rusty
point. After wiping it clean on his hair he put the pen back in
the penholder beside the ink bottle.

The office contained only a table of unfinished wood, two

equally unpainted upright chairs, and two long benches against the wall. He looked at the benches and regretted that there were no accused or litigants seated on them, whose lives or property he could interfere with to his own advantage.

Then he went outside and looked across toward the village, holding out his hand to feel the direction of the wind. He rounded the corner of the building; from here he could see the boys, who were cackling like a flock of geese in front of the schoolroom door. He called out from the corner, "Ahora, muchachos, escuela—time for school now, boys." The boys immediately lined up in front of the door.

"Atención!" he commanded.

Some of the boys, who had learned their lessons on previous days, cried out shrilly, "Buenos días, señor Profesor."

Don Gabriel spent the next half hour calling them to attention, bringing them into some semblance of order, and teaching them the jubilant "Buenos días, señor Profesor"—all of which had to be repeated each time he approached the schoolroom door to show that school had begun.

He had to put them through it every day because every day there were new arrivals who were not acquainted with the routine. Don Gabriel considered this to be the most important lesson he could give them. It cost him the least possible mental exertion, and with this slight outlay of intellect he achieved an immediate and visible result, something which could never have followed so quickly from endeavoring to hammer the alphabet into their heads.

At the same time it was something impressive to show any officials who might come along on a tour of inspection. If any such caballeros put in an appearance the whole school would jump to attention at the word of command. It might even happen that the jefe político would come in person, and the señor Jefe Político would be delighted to see how smoothly the wheels of discipline revolved. He would take it as a compliment to him-

self and recognize that the boys were being brought up to respect his authority. The dictator would have no need to fear
that when they grew up they would be rebellious and demand
their rights, if the machinery worked so well at a simple word
of command. Once this was drilled into them in their youthful
years, the dictator or the archbishop had only to shout "Atención!" and they would all forget that they had come to claim
their rights and liberties.

The boys enjoyed springing to attention and lining up and
shouting much more than sitting quietly in school. It was also
a good beginning for the learning of Spanish. The boys knew
only the speech of their Indian fathers and mothers, and as the
Tseltals have no word for attention, this was a first introduction
to the language of their country.

Don Gabriel had to explain everything first in the children's
own speech. He spoke it very badly, to say the least, and anyone less polite and tactful than Indians are would have gone
into fits of laughter at every word he said. But these children
were too well brought up by their parents to make a grown-up
person look ridiculous, even though he stuttered and had no
roof to his mouth.

When they were able to bellow "Buenos días, señor Profesor" to their teacher's satisfaction, he taught them to say
"caballero" instead of "señor Profesor." They were taught to
use that form of address whenever it was a question of anyone
but their teacher. "Caballero" was right on all occasions. It
could even be used in addressing clerics, about whose titles don
Gabriel was not very clear.

4

Neither the schoolroom nor any other room in the cabildo had
a window. There was only the door, and this, as with all the
other rooms of the building, had to be left open if daylight
was to be admitted.

Not a house in the villages or small towns of Mexico, whether a dwelling or a place of business or an office, has windows; the majority of houses even in towns of medium size are without windows, and there are thousands of windowless houses in the larger towns, particularly in the poor sections. At night the doors are securely bolted and people sleep in the atmosphere of a vault. After living for a time in Mexico you get so used to it that you quite forget that a house can have windows. During the day the climate enables you to leave the door open all the year through, and so windows are not missed.

The floor of the schoolroom, as of all the other rooms, was of beaten earth. The roof was of palm leaves. There was no ceiling beneath them.

The furniture consisted of a very small wooden table and a rickety chair. There were no benches or desks for the pupils, who had either to stand or to squat on the ground.

On the table was the one and only book the school possessed. Its title was *What a Farmer Must Know in Order to Keep His Stock in Health*. This book had presumably been left behind by a former secretary. It was in tatters and must already have served as a plaything for the pupils of several secretaries. There was once another book; it was in so sorry a plight that it scarcely deserved the name now, even if half of it had not been missing. The missing pages had no doubt been given to a passing official who was not accustomed to using tufts of grass for his private needs. Its condition was all the worse because the edges of the pages that remained had been gnawed by roaches and mice. Its title was *Popular Astronomy*.

There was also a small bottle of congealed ink on the table, and beside it in a penholder a pen with a rusty point. To the left of these items were a few sheets of paper. The children were supplied with neither pencils nor paper.

The village schools appeared in the statistics with imposing figures of attendance so that the world should know that Mexico marched in the forefront of civilized peoples. But the schools had no benches, no desks, no pencils, no pens, ink, books, paper, and no qualified teachers. This was not mentioned in the statistics, nor did anyone require that it should be mentioned. This is how it comes about that in all spheres of human activity it is far easier to lie and deceive statistically than nonstatistically. It is only necessary to omit from your statistics whatever might lessen their effectiveness. If with all these schools and such a high percentage of attendance and after thirty years of dictatorship, 50 per cent of the people could neither read nor write, it was not the fault of the dictator. You cannot fill brains with a funnel. If the children learned nothing, the fault was theirs; and it only showed how necessary it was to maintain the dictatorship and the power of the Church in view of the incapacity of the Indians for learning anything, for acquiring knowledge, and for governing themselves.

5

Behind the table in the schoolroom two boards taken from old boxes were nailed up on the wall. Don Gabriel took a piece of chalk and wrote an A and said, "That is an A. What is it now?" The children shouted all together, "An ayee."

Then he chalked up B and said, "That is B. What is it?"

The children shouted, "A bee."

By the time he reached H he felt exhausted. "Now we'll have a break. You can play outside, but don't start beating one another or I'll beat you with this bean stick, you cochinos. That's what you are, pigs. What are you?"

"Cochinos," the children shouted in chorus.

"You know that, at least," he said.

He went into the living quarters and poured himself some brandy. Then he sought out his wife and made up with her. As they slept in the same bed and he had the night to think of, he thought it best to be reconciled while there was yet time. One ought always to be reconciled with one's wife before the sun sets, particularly if there is no one else at one's disposal. But it was a long time till sunset, and before a typical day was done they were to have, perhaps, four more bitter quarrels. Nevertheless, he contrived each time to make his peace again, and because the last reconciliation took place as he blew out the candle, there was no time left for a fifth quarrel, and peace was maintained until morning. War broke out again before breakfast, and so they were able to start the new day in a state of matrimonial felicity. It would be impossible to endure marriage without these daily battles, and if they were lacking, something else would have to take their place. For the life of man is attack, and of woman counterattack with artillery support from concealed positions in her rear and a constant massing of reserves.

After an hour's break don Gabriel went back to his teaching. He began with "Atención" and the beating of two boys who were pulling each other's hair. They ran home howling to tell their fathers.

Don Gabriel did not worry about that. His duty was merely to open a school and to keep it open. Besides, five new boys had appeared, so the loss was made up for. As three others had gone home to their huts during the break and had not returned, the number of scholars remained the same.

He pointed now to the A. "What is that?"

"An eff," shouted the majority, while two maintained with heat that it was a D.

Don Gabriel shook his head in despair. "Wrong," he said. "It is an A."

"An ayee," the boys shouted.

"What is this?" he asked, pointing to the B.

"An ayeech," shouted some, while others said an E.

Don Gabriel's despair deepened and he realized that a teacher's life was no joke. "You donkeys will never learn it as long as you live. It's useless. It would need a crowbar to get it into your Indian skulls."

Now he wrote an I. "That is an I. Say it, all of you."

"That is an Ieee, say it all of you," the boys shouted with joy.

"Curse you," he cried in a rage. "You have to say I only and nothing else."

"Ieee," shouted the boys.

They were all crowded around the table and don Gabriel next wrote a J on the board. At this point, one of the boys called out, "I know that. It's a tethered goat and my father told me I had to go home now to keep an eye on the goats in case they got into the maize."

"You'll stay here," don Gabriel said. The boy began to cry.

"Oh, get off with you and go to hell," don Gabriel shouted. "But mind you're here for school first thing in the morning or you'll have the bean stick broken over your back."

The boy ran out and don Gabriel said, "It is a J, but you'll never learn it. What's the use of my bothering with you any longer, shouting my lungs out. We'll go on to something else. Now listen: I am a Mexican, viva Mexico, viva, arriba!"

The boys shouted it out after him and don Gabriel said, "You know that now and don't forget it."

The children had no idea what it meant, for don Gabriel did not bother to explain it in their own tongue. But this "viva Mexico" and "up with Mexico" gave him a new idea as to the course his instruction might take.

He had had no plan, nor the least notion of how children ought to be taught. He had merely been prepared to write the letters on the board and to give them their names. If the children remembered them, they would have learned to read; if they did not remember them, it would not have been his fault. His duty as a teacher would have been done once he had told them what the letters were called. He had not known what else might be done and at that point his capacities as a teacher would have been exhausted.

But this "viva Mexico" was an inspiration. He now saw clearly what line to take. "Listen carefully, muchachos," he said, "I am going to sing you something and you will then sing it after me."

He began to sing the national anthem. He sang it so badly that it might have been a fox trot, and when he got to the third line he was stuck and could get no farther. He had to be content, therefore, with singing the first two lines over and over again; and then the children had to sing them after him. They bawled them out without understanding a word, since the words were of course in Spanish.

Don Gabriel found this an admirable method for carrying out the primary object of the school, which was to teach these Indian children the language of their country. When the children had droned out the two lines a dozen times he was satisfied with the success he had achieved, although no one who had not been carefully forewarned could have said whether the boys were singing in Spanish or Hindustani.

He waited now for a new inspiration, and then it occurred to him that he might make use of the children in order to secure a better post for himself in the government service. His new idea was to teach them the oath of allegiance to the flag. He knew that no official who chanced to come along on a tour of inspection would ever go to the trouble of finding out whether the children could read or write. It would be too exhausting, and boring besides. Officials do not want to be bored. But an admirable impression would be made when he called the boys to attention if they cried out in Spanish "Good morning, caballero" and sang a line or two of the national anthem; and if in addition they recited the oath of allegiance to the flag—in Spanish, of course—the inspector would see at once that don

Gabriel deserved promotion and was the very man for the post even of tax collector, if there happened to be a vacancy.

So don Gabriel added the oath to his curriculum. But when he began to say it he found that here too he could not get far. He was so uncertain of the second sentence that he gave it up and contented himself with teaching them the opening words and making them repeat the first two lines of the national anthem.

He was convinced that this would afford an ample demonstration of the progress the school was making. No official would ever expect to hear the oath repeated in full or want to hear every verse of the national anthem sung. On the contrary, he would be thankful to don Gabriel for sparing him the necessity of listening to the rigmarole in all its tedious length in this filthy Indian village. It would show his tact if he merely gave the official an idea of the curriculum and its successful results. He might even say, in order to avoid any suspicion of negligence, that he was merely giving a sample and that he knew that the señor Comisario's or the señor Inspector's time was too valuable, and that he could not expect him to listen hour after hour while the children repeated and sang all they had learned.

Don Gabriel knew what he was about. When some months later a tax inspector passed through and, in order to show an excess of zeal, included an inspection of the school in the report of his tour, don Gabriel pulled it off exactly as he had planned. The following note appeared in the inspector's report: "Visited and inspected in an unofficial capacity the village school conducted by the local secretary, señor Gabriel Orduñez. Very promising and satisfactory in all respects. All the children speak Spanish and are well advanced in reading, writing, and history."

This report, like all other such reports, told the truth. Statistics and reports assume great importance under a dictatorship or a despotism. They are the façade of the structure and there must not be so much as a scratch on the gilding. And nowhere are people, whether in an official or private capacity, so clever at running up façades as under a dictatorship, where everyone who wishes to live unmolested, or even to live at all, has at all costs, and whatever else he may say or do, to plaster up a stucco front in case he incurs the suspicion of not seeing eye to eye with the political regime.

After don Gabriel had taught school for two or three weeks he found that his pupils were still not sure whether the letter he chalked up was an A or a G. He told them ten times a day that they would never learn it even if they came to school for a hundred years. The boys agreed with him, and so they came to school only when they did not know what else to do. There was never a day when more than a quarter of them were present.

Don Gabriel then hit on a new method, though really it was not his own discovery. He had seen it in practice in another place when as a cattle dealer he had been buying animals through the secretary there. This method now occurred to him and he adopted it with a slight improvement on the patent.

He collected useless scraps of paper from the store, torn wrappings and the margins of newspapers. Then he wrote a short sentence on each of the scraps of paper in ink: The cow is brown and has four legs; The goat has horns and a tail; Sheep are black or white and have wool; The tree is tall and has many branches; The secretary is a caballero and has a wife; The governor rules the state uprightly and well; The president of the country is a general and a good and wise man; The Mexican Republic has a famous president, don Porfirio; The jefe político of our district is an honorable man and re-spected by all; The Mexicans are the best fighters in the world and a noble people; The sun is in the sky and is round; My father has a field and goats and sheep.

When he had inscribed a sufficient number of bits of paper in this manner, he gave one to each of the boys and showed him how to hold it in the correct position for reading the sentence written on it. "Always hold it so that the thumb of your right hand comes on this spot. Look, like this."

Then he read the sentence over and the boy had to repeat it until he knew it by heart. The boy was given only a rough idea of what the sentence meant as a whole. He was not told which word meant sheep and which goat. All he could do was gabble out the words without knowing either the sense of them or distinguishing one word from another.

He was then left with his piece of paper and instructed to keep on rattling off the words he had learned by heart, without break or pause, looking all the time at the paper in his hand. Don Gabriel meanwhile took on the next boy and repeated the process, until he too could reel off his sentence.

Finally every boy had had his scrap of paper gone over with him; and all of them rattled off their lines, of which don Gabriel was the author and begetter, as hard as they could in a wild babble of voices.

For the next weeks the curriculum consisted almost entirely in repeating every day the two lines which don Gabriel knew of the national anthem and in reciting the sentences which each boy had on his own scrap of paper. This went on for four or five hours, with a number of breaks—during which the boys romped about outside and don Gabriel retired to drink some brandy.

And, sure enough, one day don Casimiro, the jefe político of the district, arrived on a tour of inspection.

After the boys had been called to attention and had bawled out their "Buenos días, caballero," they repeated the first two lines of the national anthem in a singsong which had no resemblance at all to the tune. But don Casimiro did not mind that. Nor did it strike him that these two lines were all they knew, for as soon as they had rattled them off they shouted out, "I am a Mexican, viva México, arriba México!"

All this convinced don Casimiro that, in the matter of education, the utmost to be expected of Indian children was already achieved.

Then the boys stepped forward, one after the other with their bits of paper in their hands, and rattled off their sentences. The jefe político looked at a few of the bits of paper and saw to his great satisfaction that the boys read what was actually written.

In return for don Gabriel's tactfulness in not wearying him too long with this demonstration, don Casimiro was equally tactful in not requiring that one boy should read what was written on his neighbor's paper. He did not summon a boy and point to a particular word and ask, "What is this word here?" Nor did he single a boy out and say, "Show me the word maize in this sentence."

Next don Gabriel had his pupils count from one to twenty. And finally he asked: "What is Mexico?" The children shouted in chorus: "Mexico is a free and independent republic."

"Who is at the head of the Mexican Republic?" he asked, and the children shouted: "A president." "What is his name?" "General don Porfirio."

With this the proceedings came to an end. Don Casimiro shook don Gabriel's hand and told him that he was extremely pleased with the result. In his report he stated that the boys of the place, under the instruction of a secretary whom he himself had chosen for his outstanding ability, could all speak and read and write Spanish and knew their figures.

The school appeared in the annual statistics as a village school of maximum efficiency, to which was added the note: "Ages from seven to fourteen. No illiterates."

Hundreds of Indian villages which were situated at distances of between eighty and four hundred kilometers from the nearest railroad were awarded an equally flattering mention in the returns; for no jefe político was so lacking in zeal as to yield the first place to another. Not even Denmark could boast such statistics, and the dictator's fame as the educator of his people and a zealous protector of the Indian race was assured for all time. For the statistics were carefully printed on the best of paper and splendidly bound, and were dispatched to the governments of every civilized nation.

"What a promising country," said the American bankers. And they gladly lent millions to the American-owned railroad companies, to the light and power companies, the mining companies, the oil companies, the development companies, and the rubber companies, so as not to be behind in the exploitation of a country with so great a future, where the Mexican had as little political liberty or economic scope as a Chinese in Australia and where the Indian was no less a slave than the proletarian Negro in Liberia.

3

 Don Gabriel's great sorrow was that the school brought him no monetary return.

He had succeeded during all the weeks he had spent in the village in bringing off all sorts of deals by a discreet exercise of his authority. There had been special levies on dealers, special levies on animals the Indians slaughtered in the village, special levies on family celebrations which the Indians of the village held among themselves, fines on brandy which the Indians brought back with them when they had been to a town to market and had not been able to conceal from don Gabriel— particularly when their drunkenness gave the show away.

It was not don Gabriel's intention to spend the rest of his life as secretary in this Godforsaken place. The task he had set himself was to make his money there as quickly as he could and then to buy himself a large farm—a finca—or to start a brandy distillery in a town.

If God bestows a job on anybody, he must not tempt God and make a fool of Him. He must make the very most of the favor shown him, remembering that he is unworthy to appear in God's presence, and so profiteer with a dollar that it becomes ten. But don Gabriel was not fertile in ideas which might have hastened this happy process.

However, it happened that his younger brother Mateo came to visit him in the nick of time.

2

Don Mateo's visit was not entirely of his free choice. He had no particular affection for don Gabriel and he did not care whether his brother's affairs went well or ill.

Mateo had always been lucky—or, since luck is not easy to define, it is more exact to say that he had the faculty of choosing for his friends only those who would be of personal service to himself. By means of these useful connections he had run through a whole series of good jobs—postmaster in a small town, inspector of weights and measures, locust warden, inspector of slaughterhouses, market overseer. From this last post he had at one bound secured the most coveted of all jobs the dictatorship had to offer—that of tax collector.

No post, not even that of inspector of schools or commissioner of health, demanded knowledge of any kind. Illiterates might be generals. Anyone who was acquainted with the effects of castor oil and was quite sure that the majority of people had their hearts on the left side could be an army doctor and put what letters he liked after his name. Offices were created not for the benefit of the people but as a provision for those who considered don Porfirio the greatest statesman of the last four centuries, or to line the pockets of those who might otherwise use their influence as members of rich and powerful families to make things unpleasant for the ruling coterie.

When it was considered that a tax collector had had plenty of time to make his pile, and when in spite of ample warning he did not retire in favor of another who was eager to make his fortune, it frequently happened that he became involved in a brawl, usually on some festive occasion when a good deal of drink was put away. The man was purposely insulted and provoked until he pulled out his revolver. This was the signal to shoot him in self-defense. In this way his post became vacant; and the man who had shot him was usually his successor. As the judge, the chief of police, the mayor, and the witnesses were all in the game with the man who was to have the job, the murder was forgotten as soon as the tax collector who had met his end in this unfortunate and regrettable manner had been buried with every mark of esteem. The new tax collector gave a large dinner party and a smart ball.

A tax collector had an adequate salary, but he treated it merely as pocket money. The receipts that made the office such a coveted one came from other sources.

First of all, he received a good percentage of all taxes he collected. The object of this was to interest him in his job and ensure that he would squeeze the utmost that could be squeezed out of the industry of the country. Before an enterprising manufacturer could start to weave a thousand yards of cotton he had to pay out the value of twenty-five yards in licenses and taxes. The government was not interested in Mexicans building up industries of their own in their own country. It suited it better to make a profit out of the high tariffs on imported goods and to stand well with American, English, and French export houses; and the high import figures were a proof of the golden age introduced by the dictator.

A tax collector also had other means of adding to his income. He had the right to assess the tax for every branch of industry and for every vocation and for every income. There was some justification for this. In so large a country it was scarcely possible to lay down a flat rate by one legal enactment. Districts which were far from rails and roads had higher transport costs; in some districts the cost of living was high, in others low; in one place wages and overhead charges were low, in another high.

If the state administration computed the tax on a brandy distillery at two hundred pesos a month on the basis of its output, the collector might on grounds of his own put it at four hundred pesos. Then the manufacturer paid him a visit. He maintained that it was impossible for him to pay such a high monthly tax. The upshot was that he gave the collector a thousand pesos; in return the collector put him down for a monthly tax of two hundred and fifty. There was the additional advantage that the collector got the credit for exacting fifty pesos more than the state had reckoned on.

The manufacturer could, of course, have disputed the tax by legal means. But he would have had to pay for a year or even longer at the rate assessed, and then months and months would have gone by before the appeal was heard. Even if the higher authorities decided in his favor it might have been another year or longer before he recovered the amount he had paid in excess. As the manufacturer would have had to pay all the costs of the hearing and engage a lawyer in the town where the appeal was heard, his expenses would have eaten up most of what he could have hoped to recover. So even if he had been successful, the sum that would finally have come into his hands would not have been worth talking about.

Usually, too, it turned out that he had in fact paid less tax than he ought to have paid. This would have been revealed in the course of hearing the appeal, since an investigation into his affairs would have been included. For these reasons it was in all cases simpler for the taxpayer to come to terms with the tax collector and leave him to his pickings. It was both cheaper and safer in the long run.

It is easy to see, therefore, why the post of tax collector was so eagerly coveted and why a runner-up did not scruple to put the occupant of it out of the way if he did not vacate it of his own accord when his time was up.

3

The town in which don Mateo, with the help of influential friends, had secured his post as tax collector was only a small one. But even this little job was a source of satisfaction to a man who had no other means of support, just as don Gabriel welcomed the post of a local secretary, miserable though it was, as an opportunity of getting on his feet.

Then one day there was to be an audit and don Mateo was more than three thousand pesos short. He tried to borrow the money but failed. Whereupon he hit on a remarkable expedient—one, however, which though remarkable was not without precedent.

Don Mateo started out on horseback to a remote part of his district to collect taxes. On the next day but one he returned without his horse, in a sorry state and with a gun wound in his arm. He went to the chief of police and told him that he had been attacked by bandits on the way home and robbed of all the money he had on him—more than three thousand pesos. His horse made its way home that night, with a bloodstained saddle.

Even so, his accounts did not balance when it came to the audit. He had not been clever enough to disguise the fact that the three thousand pesos which he said he had collected and been robbed of were the same as the three thousand pesos of which he could give no account. But the auditors, who knew next to nothing of bookkeeping and had only become auditors because they wanted some job or other and no other was available, were not up to the task of bringing the deficiency home to don Mateo. They contented themselves with the assertion that the three thousand pesos of which he had been robbed were the same three thousand pesos as those which were missing.

As one of the auditors had a friend to whom he owed a good turn and for whom he had long since promised to find a job, he took the opportunity of suggesting to don Mateo that he should resign his post of his own accord. Don Mateo did not need a second hint and sent in his resignation.

From that time onward he did next to nothing. He kicked up his heels in Balún-Canán, ran after women, tried a few deals selling houses and farms, bought and sold horses and mules off and on, and supported his friends in their fights for office in the municipalidad and in the district in the hope that if one of his friends got a job something would then turn up for him too.

There was a fierce conflict during the canvassing for the election of the presidente of the municipalidad and the rival gangs began a shooting match. Don Mateo had the misfortune to plug the chief of police, who was on the other side, in the right leg with a .45 bullet. The misfortune was in the bullet, for while none of the others exchanged on that occasion could be traced to their source, the chief of police knew for certain who it was to whom he owed the .45. And as the party to which he belonged was for the moment in power, there was nothing for don Mateo to do but to be on horseback and to take the road for Guatemala while his friends covered his retreat.

Everybody in those parts who on account of any indiscretion has to flee for his life makes for Guatemala, where he is neither picked up nor handed over for deeds done in Mexico; so the chief of police was pretty sure that don Mateo would not fail to do the same.

The road is a good one as far as the lakes, but it is no better for the pursuers than for the pursued. Beyond the lakes there is nothing but a Godforsaken jungle trail as far as the first village in Guatemala. Don Mateo had had a good start, but it was the jungle he was afraid of.

His pursuers had orders to call on him to halt when they came in sight of him, and if he did not halt to shoot him down. Don Mateo knew what he could expect. He knew that he would be shot on sight whether he halted or not—naturally. The chief of police was his bitterest enemy—because of a certain woman to start with, and in addition because it was known that don Mateo hoped to be chief himself if his gang came out on top. In that case the chief would have had to leave the town, for Mateo would have found some pretext for doing him in in self-defense.

Because he was afraid of the long and lonely ride through the jungle, and because, too, he felt that his horse began to weary, Mateo altered his plan. He turned aside and headed north, skirting San Antonio and Las Margaritas. He rested at Santa Helena, continued on his way up to Santa Rita, skirted Hucutsín, where he was known and where there was a telephone, and landed at his brother's in Bujvilum.

There he was almost as safe as in Guatemala. He was in another district; and if anyone were to pass through who knew him he could hide. No one would dream of looking for him there, because everyone would believe him to be in Guatemala.

In three months the wound in the chief's leg would have healed and been forgotten. Don Mateo could then return and lie low until such time as his own gang was in the saddle again.

In Mexico people are not cantankerous over these occurrences. If you keep out of the way and give time for the blood to cool and the wound to heal, you can be sure of being left in peace; that is, until you plug a fellow afresh.

4

Don Gabriel had no great love for his brother Mateo. Mateo was quarrelsome and self-opinionated, forever boasting of his superior knowledge and abilities and never missing a chance of putting down his brother and belittling whatever he might try to do.

"I can be a big help to you in your job here," said don Mateo.

"Well," replied don Gabriel, "there's not a lot to help me with. There's nothing to do. All that has to be done in a year I could do in a day without exerting myself."

"What do you get out of the school, then?" asked Mateo.

"Not a cent," said don Gabriel. "I just do it for the sake of doing something. Looks well, too, in the report and if anybody comes along. It's thrown in for the few pesos a month I get as secretary."

Don Mateo laughed indulgently. "I never did think you very bright, Brother, but I didn't think it was as bad as that. The school should bring you in thirty or even fifty pesos a month."

"The parents don't pay for their children's schooling."

"I didn't suppose so," Mateo said. "But by law the children have to attend school—every day. And if they don't come, why shouldn't you fine the fathers a peso—or three pesos?"

"That's true," don Gabriel allowed. "I never thought of that." Since only about thirty boys came to school on any one day and ninety stayed away, it did not take long to see that this could put ninety pesos in his pocket.

"Not to have it too steep for a start," don Mateo went on, "you needn't even make it a peso. Two reales—twenty-five centavos—for every absentee——"

"That's a damned good notion," said don Gabriel.

5

He lost no time in putting his brother's advice into action. That very afternoon he let it be known that he would have to hold a meeting of the village council the next day, as there were matters of importance to discuss; he requested the presence of the casique and his councilors. To carry through such an unpopular measure he needed the help of the Indian jefe, as he had before over the sale of the animals.

The next morning the jefe and his councilors came to the cabildo. Don Gabriel invited them to come in and asked them to sit down on the bench. Don Mateo was there too, and don Gabriel said briefly, "This is my brother who has come to pay me a visit."

Don Gabriel fumbled about among the printed regulations which lay on the table, then picking up one at random began thus: "This is a new regulation just issued by the government."

The jefe and his three supporters exchanged glances, which, however, revealed less than was in their minds. They knew from experience that whenever a new government regulation arrived, it meant either money to pay or unpaid labor to provide for the making of a road in some district remote from their own—in which, therefore, they had not the slightest interest.

The regulation don Gabriel had in his hand was concerned with the duty of all secretaries to make a regular inspection of telephone wires, and included a number of instructions showing how minor disturbances on the line could easily be remedied by the secretaries themselves and the line kept in working order.

Neither don Gabriel nor any secretary throughout the state ever dreamed of bothering his head with this regulation or thought of inspecting the telephone wires. The government, though it circulated this and many other such regulations to the secretaries, did not for a moment expect them to. All these documents were issued simply so that someone in an office, who had to be occupied in one way or another, might fill in his time by elaborating on them after the months of arduous toil spent in their formulation. They had another object too: when it came to placing the order for the printing of them, a higher official could make something out of it by coming to terms with the printer and arranging for a small hiatus between the sum the printer received and the sum for which he gave a receipt.

Don Gabriel held this regulation aloft and then went over to the jefe and put it into his hand. Neither the jefe nor any of his council could read, but there were some diagrams on the document, designed to show how to make temporary repairs on broken wires and how the wire had to be fastened to the insulators so as to prevent leakage of current.

Don Gabriel pointed to a diagram and said, "It says here that I have to let the government know by the telephone when anything is not done as the government orders."

The Indians took this in, for they actually saw the drawing of the telephone wire.

"The government says here in this regulation," don Gabriel went on, "that every boy in the place must come to school every day except Saturday and Sunday, when all schools are closed throughout the whole Republic. And the government lays it down that for every day a boy does not come to school his father must pay a fine of a peso to the secretary of the place."

The Indians did not utter a word. They merely nodded several times and looked at their jefe, who nodded likewise.

The jefe rolled a cigarette and then said, speaking slowly, "We cannot pay that. We have not the money. Many a father here has six children—how can he pay six pesos a day when his boys are getting big and have to work with him on the land when the maize is being sown, or when the boys have to stay with the sheep in case a jaguar takes the lambs?"

"Yes, that's true," don Gabriel allowed, "but I can do nothing. I am only the secretario. It is the government's order and I must do as the government says or else I shall be put in prison."

Don Mateo now joined in the discussion. "It is the same everywhere in the state. It is the same at Balún-Canán and at Jovel."

The casique looked at him and said very slowly, "Are you secretary here?"

"No, of course not," don Mateo said, rather taken aback by the unexpected question, "but I know it is so everywhere."

"No doubt you brought this regulation along with you?"

"Yes," replied don Mateo unconvincingly. "I was on the way here to visit my brother, and so the postmaster gave me the letter to bring along."

The jefe rose, and his advisers stood up at the same time. "Then we can go now," he said, "unless you have another regulation there?"

"No," said don Gabriel, "there was only this one."

Next day, as usual, only about thirty boys came to school. Don Gabriel began to write down the names of the fathers of the boys who were absent, so as to be able to collect a peso for each of them. But here he came up against a blank wall, the existence of which he had not anticipated.

He had a list of all the hundred and twenty boys in the place, but in most cases the names were those he had given them himself, so as to be able to include them in his report. It was only in a very few cases that he knew their fathers, and in these cases it was because they lived in the village. The majority of the Indian families were scattered about the countryside. Some lived right in the jungle.

He could think of no way of finding out the names of the fathers whose boys were absent that day—nor of those whose boys would be absent the next. As even Mateo was at a loss for advice in this predicament, he began to lose all hope of any private gain from the school; and this was one of the principal reasons for a decline in the interest don Gabriel took in it.

6

Two weeks later the cura, the priest for the district, passed through the place. The Indians came with their wives and children to kiss the cura's hand. In return he gave them his apostolic blessing, and with that his labors in the pueblo were at an end.

The arrival of the cura brought a blessing to the house of the secretary too, a blessing which took a tangible form.

Don Gabriel's wife let it be known in the village that she had nothing in the house and yet she must offer the señor Cura hospitality: the saintly man must certainly not be left to starve. Two hours later don Gabriel had eight hens, fourteen eggs, six turkeys, two suckling pigs, five kids, and the meat of a deer in his larder. The saintly man could not possibly eat all this, and what was left did not come amiss to don Gabriel.

The school was paraded for the señor Cura's benefit and he was extremely pleased with the progress it was making.

"I know, señor Secretario," he said to don Gabriel as they sat together after dinner, "what a hard task you have here and it does one good to see the success of your efforts."

"Gracias, señor Cura," replied don Gabriel modestly, "I thank you. I could do far, far more in the way of education if only the attendance were regular."

The holy man nodded sympathetically and patted his stomach. "I don't know what it is, but I think it is just here, on the liver. No—here," and he guided don Gabriel's hand toward the organ referred to. "It may be the kidneys," he went on, "I'm not quite sure. But I have frequent indigestion. And I don't sleep well either. I suppose you haven't such a thing as a glass of good old comiteco in the house, señor Secretario? Thank you, thank you. It is a cordial. There is nothing like the tequila of Comitán—the best in the country. Yes, yes, another, if you please. No, no, fill it up and have no fear—two glasses don't put me under the table. As for the attendance—don't mind what the government says. What does the government know about it? The authority lies with the father. That is God's law and God's will—since the beginning of the world.

And if the father needs the boy's work, it is the duty of the child to obey his father. That is God's will, and it is not for us men to interfere with the will of God, Who knows what is for the best. If a child learns to be obedient to his father and to God, what more or what better can we poor sinners teach him? A wise government is one that sows no discord between father and child. Obedience to a father is of more account than obedience to any earthly government. Let the children here come to school if and when they like; their own fathers know what is good for them. What good can it do to strip these folk of their childlike innocence, to cram them with reading and writing and to upset their happy lives with the idle rubbish called knowledge? Rubbish, idle rubbish, that's all it is. The Kingdom of Heaven stands open to the innocent and the ignorant— whether to others also is a matter for doubt, for nothing has been said about that. Yes, if you please, another glass, with pleasure. Yes, fill it to the top. It aids the digestion. Mine is sluggish and jibs at every turn. As I said before, señor Secretario, let the children come to school when and how they like. To tell the truth, I'm against village schools altogether, as the Right Reverend the Lord Bishop is also. The fewer the better: none at all, best of all. But in spite of that I recognize all you have done in these few months for the education of the children. It is wonderful how far advanced they are. It does you great honor. Salud—your health! Well, perhaps just one more, but only one, the very last. It's excellent. How is the road to Tanquinvits just now? Very soft? I was bogged down there two years ago. My old mule and I were in it up to the middle."

"You can ride it quite well at this time of year," said don Gabriel. "There are a few places where caution is necessary, where you have stones covered with mud and slime and holes between them. It is best, señor Cura, to dismount then. A mule may get a leg between two stones and easily break it. But there's less danger if you get off. The beast can free itself more easily when it has no weight on its back."

The cura pondered a moment while he lit a cigarette, and then said, "The people in your district here are very kindly and industrious folk. The thing is just to leave them in peace. They are like children and they must be treated like children. And if they get drunk now and then, don't say a word to them. They sleep it off by the next day."

Don Gabriel got up. "Excuse me, señor Cura, I have a letter or two to write. I was going to ask whether you would take them with you to Jovel and post them there."

The holy man laughed. "It will be a week or ten days before I get to Jovel. I'm visiting every little place in the district. I don't hurry. My mule ambles along like an old broken-down piebald and I let her go at her own pace. God's affairs move slowly and need no flying machines. Have you ever seen those machines? I don't believe in them. And nothing will come of them. Man should not try to improve on God. If God had wished us to fly in the air He would have given us wings. And by not giving us wings but reserving them for the angels, He has clearly told us His will and we ought to obey it. If your letters are not in a great hurry I will take them gladly."

"There's no hurry with them," answered don Gabriel, "but it is a chance of getting them off."

"Yes, I'll take one more glass with pleasure," said the cura. "I don't often come across such a good añejo, so properly aged, and it does me good. It warms up the stomach. But it must be the very last. And then, with your kind permission, I will lie down."

7

Next day, when the priest had ridden off with his boy, don Gabriel said to his brother, "That tip of yours was no good at all. There's nothing to be made out of the school. I don't want to have the Church about my ears."

"If you don't want to make what you can here, that's your own lookout," don Mateo replied with indifference. "It's no concern of mine."

"I always thought you were so smart and knew everything better than I did," said don Gabriel.

This observation rankled—all the more because Mateo, being alone there with his brother and his sister-in-law, had nothing else to occupy his mind. He had always maintained that he owed his luck in getting good jobs to his abilities, which were greater than those of other men, and that his older brother in particular was a fool beside him. In their daily quarrels he came back again and again to his contention that if he had been secretary there for six months it would have been a very different story and that in two years he could put at least five thousand pesos in his pocket.

"I'd very much like to know," don Gabriel said every time, "where you'd get your five thousand pesos from in a place like this. If you turned every family here inside out you wouldn't find three hundred pesos among the lot. The people just don't have it. It is easy to say five thousand in two years. It's another matter in a place such as you were in where there are three brandy distilleries, ten or fifteen saloons, forty shops, four restaurants, and twenty Chinese shopkeepers whom you can fleece back, front, and from all sides."

"Yes, but I wasn't the only one," don Mateo retorted. "There was the mayor, the town clerk, the tax inspector, the chief of police with six men under him, the judge, the deputies, and half a hundred more, all fleecing and squeezing at the same time. Here you are the only one to have a finger in the pie."

"Oh, damn you, shut up," don Gabriel shouted, and catching sight of the boys playing and chasing each other in front of the schoolroom door, he collared five of them and gave them a beating.

Then he heard them all say their sentences, and when that was done he had them fall in for marching and calisthenics. After that he gave them a break and came in for a glass of brandy and a quarrel with his wife.

4

 Don Gabriel was in his office. He turned over the leaflets and letters, smoothed them out, put a stone on top as paperweight, opened the ink bottle, smelled it, shook it, took up the pen and wiped it on his hair, put it down, dusted the table, and went to the door to smoke a cigarette.

Looking across by chance to where the path to the village left the bush he saw a troop of Indians on the march and about to cross the wide open space in front of the cabildo to take up the trail for Huentsingo.

Two Mexicans on horseback, each with a heavy revolver in his belt, were at the head of the troop. They called a halt for a rest and to give the stragglers time to catch up. All the Indians carried heavy packs.

The two Ladinos rode up to the portico of the cabildo. They dismounted and came up to don Gabriel.

"Buenos días," said one. "You are the secretary here?"

"Yes," said don Gabriel, "pase, come in."

"Have you any comiteco?"

"Plenty," said don Gabriel.

"Then fill our bottles," the Mexican told him. "And we'll put one down now, and one for you, señor Secretario."

61

"Thanks," said don Gabriel. "Take a seat for a moment. The brandy is in my tienda. If you or the people with you want anything for the journey, my tienda is the only one in the area. You won't find another in all the twenty kilometers you'll go today."

When he got to the store with the bottles he found his wife and Mateo busy selling tobacco, camphor, salt, chiles, cord, and other small items. About twenty of the travelers were crowded around the lowered shutter which served as the shop counter.

Don Gabriel filled the two bottles, poured three glasses of brandy, and returned to the office. They all said "Salud," and tossed down their comitecos.

"Bueno," said the men, tightening their belts as a sign that they were ready to leave. "Vámonos. We're off—we have a hard trek in front of us."

Just as they were untying their horses from the pillars of the portico, don Mateo came around the corner of the building. The Indians were all astir, hoisting up their packs and falling in.

"How many have you got with you?" don Mateo asked, just as the two men got their feet into the stirrups.

"Eighty," said one of the two as he raised himself into the saddle.

"For the coffee plantations down yonder?"

"Yes, in the Soconusco district."

"But you can't ride off just like that, caballeros," said don Mateo, stepping up to the horses' heads.

"Cómo?" asked one. "How do you mean, señor?"

"You know you have to pay passage money for them," said don Mateo, "twenty centavos a head."

"Why passage money?" the man asked. "I've paid the contract tax in full."

"That does not concern us here," said don Mateo. "We have

to charge passage money here, for the right of way. That is the
local regulation. You ought to know that as contractors of
labor, caballeros. It does not come out of your own pockets.
You charge it to these fellows' accounts as you do the tax and
the commissions you pay for them. We can refuse the right of
way unless passage money is paid."

The two agents knew that no such right existed, because
there were no bridges or causeways in the district to be kept
in repair, but they knew also that it would do them no good
if they refused to pay. They could easily with their eighty
men have overcome any opposition, but they would then have
incurred the secretary's enmity—and enmity in that quarter
would have been embarrassing. They were not only agents for
labor for the coffee plantations; they were also buyers and
sellers of animals and hides and skins, and occasionally they
might have goods to forward by pack mule. It would mean a
loss of three days if they had to avoid this village on the journey to the region of the Grijalva River, where the goods
would have to be put on board ship. It might be three years
before they had to pass through the place again; but it might
equally well be in two months. It depended on the vagaries of
business. Anyway, it was a costly matter to make an enemy of
the secretary of any place which they might have to pass
through or come to in the course of business—it was far more
advisable to have him as a friend. Every traveler, whether on
business or not, is always very much at the mercy of the local
secretary. He is the only man in the place who is not an
Indian and the only person with authority to give or withhold
protection.

The agents paid the sixteen pesos passage money. When they
asked for a receipt, Mateo said, "We haven't got the new forms
yet. But you don't need a receipt, caballeros. We won't ask
you to pay twice for the same gang."

When the party was out of sight, don Mateo turned to his

brother. "Do you see how I worked that? You'd have let them through without a word said. Whatever passes, on four legs or two, must be fleeced. That's the only way. When these fellows come back on their way home from the plantations they'll be on their own and no agent with them. Then you must take a peso apiece off them. They'll have their wages in their pockets then, and what else have they to spend their money on? And you can load them up with comiteco as well. Don't you worry about the two agents complaining of being unjustly taxed—certainly not as long as you are secretary here, and when you're not it won't matter to you; anyway, they'll have forgotten all about it by that time. And how will they know you haven't got an influential job somewhere else? They don't pay it themselves, never fear. The muchachos pay it—and they can't check on it. Their accounts are too long for that."

2

A wedding took place in the village. According to custom, the young bridegroom had to treat his own friends and the friends of both families concerned to brandy. He had already bought the brandy weeks before in Jovel, where he could buy it many times more cheaply than from don Gabriel. The cask had been secretly smuggled into the village and don Gabriel had heard nothing of it.

But since it was to be expected that a few men would get drunk, the young Indian had taken the precaution of buying ten liters from don Gabriel so that it might appear that all the brandy drunk at the wedding had come from the secretary's tienda.

"You can have more," don Gabriel told him. "It doesn't matter about paying for it now, I'll give you credit with pleasure."

But the young fellow replied that he thought he would get by on the ten liters.

All Indians are very easily and very quickly affected by brandy, particularly by the brandy sold to Indians. Many of them lose all control of themselves. Anyone who knows Indians knows this, and if he does not he finds it out quicker than is sometimes pleasant.

There was dancing without pause for two days and two nights to the music of an accordion and two guitars. The young men drank very little, and the little they drank had scarcely any effect on them owing to their indefatigability at dancing and the large quantities of coffee and even larger quantities of water they drank. Also, the young men without exception were set upon making a good impression on the girls, and particularly on their own girls. Indian girls prize sobriety in a man above good looks. They are taught by their mothers to judge men by this standard. Indian boys know this, and they know that if they lack the reputation for sobriety they will find it very hard to get the girl they want for a wife—though they may get one they don't want.

With Indians, as with other peoples, the character of a husband or a wife only begins to show itself in its true colors when there is no further need to keep up a high standard or to pretend to one; whether this happens in two weeks or two years after marriage depends on the durability and vigor of the pretense. Many married persons are so gifted at pretense that they can keep up this mutual imposture for twenty years, without either's suspecting what the other's true character is; and it sometimes occurs that the simulated character becomes in course of time and by force of habit almost the real one. That is why it so often happens that marriages of twenty-five years' standing reveal cracks, on one side or the other or on both sides at once, which no one would ever have thought possible in so harmonious a union.

It was the married men, men provided with wives and children, who found in brandy their last refuge from disillusionment. If even educated persons cannot explain why they go on pouring champagne, whisky, and cognac down their throats long after they have exhausted the impulse to arrive at self-forgetfulness or to reach a state of exaltation, it is useless asking an Indian to explain it. It is a waste of time to try to explain it at all. The best thing is simply to recognize that there are inveterate drinkers among them, as well as moderate drinkers, occasional drinkers, and total abstainers.

It was the inveterate drinkers and the occasional drinkers who made the wedding an excuse for a prolonged bout. Three of them, after they had half slept off the drunkenness of the evening before, appeared early in the morning at don Gabriel's tienda and asked for brandy. There was no more to be had at the wedding festivities because though they were kept up for days the brandy was supplied only by the members of the two families.

The men brought liter bottles with them and money too. Don Gabriel was unwilling to sell them any brandy. He was willing enough to do business, but he knew that if drunkenness got out of bounds it could mean a lot of trouble for himself.

But don Mateo came on the scene. "What does it matter to you," he said, "how much the fellows like to drink? You're not their medical adviser. All that concerns you is whether they can pay or whether, if they don't, there's money behind them."

Don Gabriel gave the men the brandy.

Two hours later wild yells were heard from the village, and an Indian woman with her baby in her arms came running to the cabildo, screaming, "He's murdered my brother and cut his head off."

Don Gabriel and don Mateo ran into the village, and there behind one of the huts they saw a crowd of men who were trying to overpower Gregorio, one of the three who had come to buy brandy that morning.

Gregorio was whirling a machete which was dripping with blood. The corpse of a boy of about eighteen was lying against the mud wall of the hut. His face was hacked up and there were deep gashes in his body.

The men, who were mostly still drunk, were trying to knock the madman over with poles, but they did not dare go near enough. They were afraid Gregorio might throw the machete.

The Indian jefe had come up as soon as he had heard the outcry, but he, too, was far from sober and looked from one to another with glazed eyes, without understanding either what was happening or what had happened.

Don Gabriel told a boy to run to his wife and ask for the lasso from his saddle. The boy was back within a few minutes. After failing in several attempts to lasso the man, don Gabriel crept around the hut and, coming on Gregorio from behind, finally succeeded in throwing the lasso over his head and bringing him to the ground. As soon as he fell several of the Indians ran up and bound him so tightly with the lasso that he could not move hand or foot. Then they carried him to the cabildo and put him in the prison. His strength was now utterly exhausted and he fell asleep.

A few drunken men, who did not know what else to do with themselves, were bellowing and carrying on in the open space in front of the cabildo. Don Mateo advised his brother to put these fellows in the prison too, in case they became a cause of further trouble. So don Gabriel summoned some men who appeared to be sober and took the fellows in charge with their help. All the women of the place and all the men who were sober agreed that don Gabriel did well to shut them up, before a second murder took place.

The inhabitants of the community, particularly the women, were in a state of panic. Four women came running to the cabildo with their children for protection against drunken husbands and brothers and spent the whole day in the schoolroom. Another woman came to don Gabriel, crying aloud and imploring him to shut up her husband because he had said he was going to kill her and her children. Don Gabriel had the man brought in and locked him up, and the woman went home with her children.

By the end of the morning peace was restored. The drunken men were apparently all asleep and the others could be seen going to their work in the fields.

3

The prison was very confined. The prisoners were packed as tight as sardines.

At midday their wives came with food for them, which they put through the bars of the stout wooden door. But not one prisoner was awake. The wives returned in the evening with more food and lit a fire in front of the door to give a little warmth during the night.

The men were still drunk. Their wives thought it safer if they remained in prison. Not one of them went to don Gabriel to ask him to release her husband. They knew, too, from previous experience and from occasions when their husbands had been locked up for drunkenness in a market town, that getting in was easier than getting out.

Next morning as soon as the sun rose the wives of the prisoners came again and squatted at the door with their infants in their laps and talked to their husbands. They put their coffeepots on the embers of the fire which had glowed all night in front of the door.

Indians are not happy at night unless they have a fire burning, or at least smoldering, at their feet. One of the women had pushed a long stick through the bars of the door, and with this, the men, whenever one of them woke from his drunken sleep and came to his right mind for a moment or two, had been able to poke more logs on the fire to keep it going.

4

Don Gabriel had not until now had an opportunity of putting anyone in prison. There had been many quarrels among the inhabitants, but no one had come to him and asked him to reconcile them. They had always been settled by the casique. Don Gabriel had no right to intervene in the affairs of the community itself. Nobody came to him when there was disagreement over the dividing of the land or a quarrel over the right to game which had been killed, or a dispute as to whether a stray kid was the offspring of Tomás's or Panfilo's goat or whether Elias was right in accusing Lino of alienating the affections of a girl he had intended to marry.

All these matters were disposed of satisfactorily by Narciso, their chief. Don Gabriel had only the right to intervene, in certain well-defined circumstances, as the representative of the government. Such a circumstance was when there was a disturbance of the peace which threatened the country and its inhabitants beyond the confines of the village itself.

His authority extended to crimes such as murder, banditry, robbery of a serious nature within the village, all robbery and attacks on the roads, and disturbances of the peace which affected the community and therefore the State. The cabildo and the space in front of it were within the jurisdiction of the State. There every citizen had the right to be unmolested. What the Indians did in their own territory, as long as it did not affect other citizens, was their own affair. Yet even here don Gabriel had the right and the duty to intervene if he were called upon. When the women of the place had been at a loss as to how to protect themselves from their drunken husbands, when their own jefe, because he was drunk himself, had been incapable of overpowering the murderer and bringing the other men to order thus averting further trouble, then they had gone to don Gabriel as their last and only resort.

It would have been easy for the young men of the place, who

were not drunk, to restore order. But it was against Indian custom for sons or young men to give orders to their fathers or to the older men of the community, and still less to enforce them. No one would bind his father or knock him down, even though his father was going to kill his mother in a fit of drunken madness. The son could only try to get his mother away and, if he could not succeed, nothing would be left but to receive the fatal blow of the machete in her stead. If a father, in a drunken fit and with his machete in his hand, called his son to him, the son would obey and be struck down without so much as lifting his arm to ward off the blow. If he was afraid that his father might try to kill him in senseless rage, he might keep out of his way; but if he heard his father's voice, or a messenger from his father found him, he would come out of his hiding place.

It was for these reasons, which lie deep in Indian custom, that don Gabriel's help had been called upon.

There were other reasons why a secretary might be asked to settle quarrels and disputes, even of a private nature. There were cases where the chief was too clever to give a decision, because he knew that whatever the decision it might bring on him the enmity not only of one man but of a whole family. In such cases he left the decision to the secretary. The secretary was accepted as impartial, since neither he nor his family nor any of his friends stood to benefit either way; for he and his possessions and his friends lay outside the community.

Such contingencies, arising inevitably from the customs and character of the Indians and their ties of blood and occupation, gave the secretaries a power and influence which lead, in the hands of corrupt officials, to the pitiless exploitation and complete enslavement of independent Indian communities.

5

Under the regime of the dictatorship the Mexican had nothing else before his eyes from childhood but an officialdom that regarded public office only as a means of enriching itself. The people were taught nothing else and they heard nothing else. If an official was spoken of, it was not "The man has a difficult and responsible post" but "The man has rounded up his sheep, he has only to shear them—he's a governor." And from early youth don Gabriel had learned that even the smallest post had to yield an income far in excess of the salary.

The dictator, don Porfirio, had astonished the world by showing in a brief space of time that the bankrupt Republic of Mexico was so flourishing that other countries could only envy its bursting treasury. It was proved by the statistics, which proved also that a great statesman had brought the Mexican people to a level of civilization and prosperity which no one would have thought possible. He knew how to keep national expenditure down to a ridiculously low figure. That was easy. Official salaries were in many cases so small that a mouse could scarcely have lived on them; and if a government inspector or a judge wanted to live in a manner befitting his station, he had to find some other source of income as well. It went without saying that he used his power to enlarge this other source to the utmost. The treasury grew richer and richer, the national debt, on paper, smaller and smaller; the poverty of the people, ignorance, corruption, and shameless injustice were, on the other hand, more and more widely diffused.

Don Gabriel knew that he was given his post as a means to enrich himself, and that he was not given it to promote the well-being of an Indian village and its inhabitants. All he lacked was the adroitness and cunning to squeeze out the last drop the job could yield.

He would never have seen that a convoy of Indian laborers

passing through the place could put sixteen pesos in his pocket if his brother Mateo had not demonstrated it. Don Mateo had a rich store of experience, gleaned from his life among other officials. It was not experience only, however, that inspired don Mateo, but—what an official needed even more—imagination and resourcefulness.

"If a job brings nothing in," he said to don Gabriel ten times a day, "then you must make it bring something in."

6

That morning, as they sat at breakfast, don Mateo said, "Well, now you have a good fat porker at last, Brother—and a milking cow too."

Don Gabriel stopped munching.

"I? Are you tipsy too? Porker and milking cow. Cómo?"

"It's a case of pearls before swine with you, hombre," don Mateo replied. "You're joking! You can't be such a blockhead as not to see the heap of pesos waiting to be picked up—the lockup full of men who want to get out, and you sitting here without a cushion to put under your hams. I believe you'd let the fat turkey escape and laugh to see it fly away into the bush. You'd let these fellows go scot-free after they've been so kind as to get themselves locked up. The luck of it—all coming of their own accord. You didn't even have to call them. They handed themselves over of their own free will."

"But I can't keep them in the lockup forever," said don Gabriel. "I'll have to let them out today or they'll smash the place down."

"Don't you worry," said don Mateo, "they won't do that. They know that will bring the soldiers along and that their houses and fields will be burned."

Before don Gabriel could reply he heard some men talking outside who were clearly waiting to see him. He put on his hat, tightened his revolver belt, and went around the corner of the building to the portico, where he found the men at the door of the office. Don Mateo buckled on his revolver and followed.

"Good morning," said don Gabriel.

The men returned the greeting.

Don Gabriel opened the door and went to his table, fumbled among his papers, uncorked the ink bottle, picked up the pen, wiped it clean on his hair, and sat down.

The men sat down on one of the benches. Don Mateo went over to the other bench and rolled a cigarette.

Then one of the men began speaking. "I am the brother of Isidro, who is in prison. This man here is the brother of Isidro's wife. And this is a half brother of Isidro's wife. And this is the brother of Isidro's father."

"And what is Isidro in prison for?" asked don Gabriel. He did not know which of his prisoners Isidro was. He knew none of them by name.

"Isidro is the man who was only drunk and shouted so much, but he meant no harm," said his brother. "We want you to let him out now. He is sober by this time, and if he doesn't see to his maize he will have a bad crop."

Don Gabriel got up. "Right," he said, "you can have him at once." He was going to let Isidro out of the prison there and then.

"Wait a bit," said don Mateo. "You must say first what multa he has to pay."

The Indians understood very little Spanish, but they understood what was being spoken of. They understood moreover that Don Mateo was interfering with the free discharge of Isidro. They were used to being threatened with a multa when for any reason, mostly drunkenness, they found themselves in prison in a town where they had gone to market. If they had no money and none of the friends or relations with them paid the fine for them, they were kept in prison for a week or longer and had to work on the roads or in the streets and parks of the town.

Here, however, they were in their own village and Isidro had done nothing but shout and refuse to go quietly to his hut.

"Isidro's multa is ten pesos," said don Mateo. "As soon as he has paid it, he can go."

"But where can Isidro get ten pesos?" asked his brother. "He hasn't got ten pesos—only a large family. Ten pesos? Why, that is nearly the price of two fat pigs when prices are good. When they are as bad as they were last time the dealers were here, it is as much as three fat pigs would bring."

"Gabriel," don Mateo called out, "isn't that what it says—ten pesos multa for drunkenness and violence?"

Don Gabriel took up a printed document. "Yes, that is laid down by the government."

"Then we cannot alter it," said don Mateo. "It is the law."

Don Gabriel had had time to grasp that a new source of income was being tapped. Now that the people of the place, having found themselves in a tight corner, had had to support the secretary—in their own defense—in arresting the drunken men, the opportunity seemed too good to lose.

It was true that don Gabriel would have let all the prisoners go without fining them if he had been alone. It would not have been because he acknowledged any responsibility for what had occurred through his having sold them the brandy, or because he had any sympathy for the weakness of the Indians, but simply from prudence.

For one thing, he was afraid. He knew what the fate of several other secretaries had been. For another thing, he did not want to force matters but rather to tap all sources gradually one by one. He was not at all as stupid as his brother supposed. At bottom he was perhaps cleverer than don Mateo; in any case, more diplomatic.

It was all very well for Mateo to take the high hand and

play the strong man. He was not responsible—he could put everything onto the secretary. And he could clear out at a moment's notice, whereas Gabriel had his wife to think of, as well as a few possessions he would not like to lose.

Gabriel had no reason to suppose that Mateo deliberately wished to get him into difficulties. He knew that Mateo had not much brotherly affection for him; all the same, he did not believe he could be so malevolent as to plan his destruction. Mateo did not covet his post—that was certain—and it was very improbable that he had an eye on his wife.

On the other hand, there was no doubt that don Mateo was a born gambler. If he was now cut off from gambling with money, he gambled with the fates of others, just to see how they turned out and to enjoy the sensation of being the power behind the scene.

7

Whatever was behind it, don Gabriel was now cornered and there was no escape. Don Mateo had named the amount of the multa and appealed to the regulations. Don Gabriel was forever debarred from saying that the multa need not be paid. He had to insist on the payment of it, whatever the consequences. Moreover, he had always counted on such fines as the chief source of revenue from his office. He had only been waiting until he was firmly in the saddle before exacting them with ruthless severity on every trivial pretext. Also, he had hoped to win over the Indian casique little by little, so as to have his support before engaging in this traffic.

But he realized that if he gave way now, once Mateo had cornered him, it would be a long time before he would be able to convince the people that fines were necessary in order to maintain peace and quiet in the place. Everyone would exclaim that he had let the worst disturbers of the peace go free, while now he was inexorable in the case of mere trivial offenders against some supposed regulation.

The decisive factor, however, was that he was afraid of Mateo's ridicule. If he did not take the tip now, he would never hear the last of it. His wife, whose avarice exceeded even his own, would add venom to every gibe of Mateo's, and he would finally have to admit that he was the biggest fool who had ever, by the grace of God, been blessed with the opportunities of office.

Don Mateo got up and took his brother aside. His manner and his lowered voice might well have suggested to the Indians present that he was pleading with his brother to show mercy to the prisoners. What he actually said, however, was this:

"Hombre, you'll never have another such chance, not if you are secretary here for a hundred years. Don't let it slip. The men and women came and begged you to put the drunks and rowdies in prison. The casique, in their view, has given his approval, since he has made no protest. Your luck again—he was as drunk as the rest. You've made your haul with the full approval of the whole place. Make them pay before they get out. After this it will go of itself. Every week you can collar one or two. There's always some pretext. You can produce as many regulations as you please—not one of them can read. If they don't like it they'll curse the government. That won't hurt you, and the government is far away. Even if they send a deputation and the governor puts himself out to receive it, they won't be able to make themselves understood, for the governor doesn't know a word of the language. He'll ask their names, shake hands, give them a meal at a fonda, some inn that serves dinners at half a peso a head, and write you an official letter telling you to find out what they want. You can say what you like in reply. In any case, he will put it to one side, for meanwhile he will have forgotten about these lousy Indians, even if

he's still governor and has not already been replaced by somebody else who knows nothing at all about the matter and is
thinking only of how much he can squeeze out of the coffee
plantations in extraordinary taxation for roads and railroads
which are never even started."

Don Gabriel knew that his brother was right. Unless he
meant to spoil his job for good, he had to grab a slice of the
pie before him.

The Indians seated on the bench had been talking too and
considering what they could do. When don Gabriel and don
Mateo turned around and faced the men again, Isidro's brother
spoke up.

"Listen, señor Secretario, we will pay four pesos for Isidro,
so that he can go back to his wife and children."

Don Mateo gave don Gabriel no time to reply. "The regulation puts the fine at ten pesos. But I am not secretary here.
If don Gabriel can put it at less, he will have to answer for it
to the government."

"Good," said don Gabriel. "I am no tirano. I am not a tyrant,
but an understanding secretario. We will say eight pesos. Isidro
is poor and he has a large family."

"Five," Isidro's brother replied to this. "We will pay five
pesos and he will be able to pay us back when he sells some
goats."

After further discussion they came to terms at six pesos multa
for Isidro.

Don Gabriel made out no receipt for the payment of the fine.
Nevertheless, don Mateo could not refrain from good advice.

"You must never give receipts, then nothing can ever be
brought home to you if the Indians here get unruly and rebel.
You must hammer it into them that the government makes these
regulations and that you are nothing but the official who is
here to carry them out and who, if he does not do so, will himself go to prison. But why make a song about it? They don't ask

for receipts. They haven't the sense. Here are the goods and there is the money, and if you give credit, another must stand surety."

"All I wonder is why they never made you a secretary," don Gabriel said with a laugh.

"Too slow for me, hombre," don Mateo replied. "I haven't your patience. I would force the pace, and then I would have them all about my ears. To tell you the truth, I wouldn't care to be on my own here with a villageful of Indians whom I was trying to fleece."

Don Gabriel threw away his cigarette and put his foot on it. "That's just what I've been thinking, Brother. You want to get me embroiled, and then you'll make yourself scarce when the sparks fly."

"That will never happen with you, Gabriel," don Mateo said, laughing. "You're too thick in the head for that. You can put a good face on it. I can't. That's why you're safe enough with a job like this."

8

By midday all but two of the prisoners had been released at six pesos a head. In some cases the money was paid in cash, in others it was entered to the prisoner's account on the surety of two of his relations.

Don Gabriel assessed the multa at twenty pesos for the man who in his drunkenness had threatened to kill his wife and children and whom his wife had begged the secretary to put in prison until he was sober again. Twenty pesos meant the value of his maize crop or twice the value of the pigs he had to sell.

His brothers and uncles and others of his family came to bargain for him. After three hours of discussion twelve pesos were agreed upon, and this sum was entered against him. All those present stood surety for payment within six weeks with three pesos interest.

No one had so far come to ask for the release of Gregorio, the murderer. Only his wife had come at regular intervals to bring him his food. Each time she squatted in front of the door of the prison, with one child at her breast and three others running here and there; and each time she sat there for three hours or more. Her husband said little to her and she less to him. She regarded it as her duty as a wife to be near her husband. Sometimes she wept silently.

In the evening she came with the baby only. She brought her husband black beans and tortillas and a jug of coffee. She lit a fire outside the door, heated the food on it, and gave it to him through the bars. She watched while he ate, and asked if he wanted salt or more water.

When he finished she handed him leaves of tobacco and he rolled himself a thick cigar. Then he leaned against the wall and smoked, asking a question now and then about affairs at home. He gave her brief instructions about the work that had to be done, and what jobs and which of the animals had to be seen to.

Then he stretched out on the straw petate his wife had brought him, covered himself with a thin and tattered blanket, and fell asleep.

His wife squatted patiently by the fire outside. She made up the fire, clasped her infant to her naked breast, smoked a cigar her husband had given her, fell asleep without stirring from the squatting position, woke up when the fire burned low, spoke gently and tenderly to her little one and clasped it more closely to her, lit the cigar again and took a few puffs, fell asleep, and woke again when the fire threatened to go out. Her husband slept peacefully; his conscience gave him no bad dreams.

When the night grew pale, the woman got to her feet and with a quick, short step returned to her hut to prepare her husband's breakfast.

9

The door of the prison was made of roughly hewn planks, which were fitted together without nails. The grating consisted of heavy pieces of wood, cut out at the intersections so that they fit into one another. Each opening was wide enough for a prisoner to put his head through if he wanted to.

The door had no lock. There was an iron staple on the doorpost, so emaciated by rust that it seemed to have galloping consumption. If anyone had put a stick through this staple and given it a twist, it would have yielded up the ghost with a faint crack and been of no further use in this world or the next.

There was a chain looped around the bar of the grating nearest the doorpost. It suffered from the same tubercular complaint as the staple. Its links were so eaten away with rust that any one of them could have been crushed between the finger and thumb.

A padlock was passed through the last link of the chain and the staple. The lock did not work, for its mechanism was rusted and immovable, but that did not enter into the question, for don Gabriel had no key. When he shut a prisoner in he merely lowered the hoop of the padlock as far as it would go. Since the works of the lock had long since fallen out of the race, there was no click to show that it had gone home. When don Gabriel released a prisoner he simply raised the hoop of the padlock.

He let the prisoner out for ten minutes or so several times a day and went into the schoolroom or to his wife in the kitchen. He had no wish to see what use the prisoner made of his liberty. As soon as the prisoner had done all he had to do, he sat down at the door of the prison and waited patiently for don Gabriel to shut him in again.

The walls of the prison, like those of the whole building of which it formed one corner, were made of thin poles, thickly daubed with mud. From inside or out they could have been broken through by a gentle kick or two. Anyone who chose could have opened the padlock as easily as don Gabriel did— every man in the place knew how it was opened and shut.

Yet, even though a prisoner might have to spend weeks in this prison waiting for sentence of death, he would not make his escape and none of his friends would have set him free.

Just as the door of a house is locked in the eyes of an Indian when it is merely tied shut with a rope, so the prison door was locked even though it could be burst open with one finger.

10

Don Gabriel considered whether there was any money to be made out of the murder, but neither he nor don Mateo saw any possibility here of increasing the secretary's receipts. It did not matter to them in the least that the man had killed a fellow Indian. Whether there are a thousand more or a thousand less of these Indians in the world makes no difference to the economic condition of Mexico; and unless they affect the income of a governor, a general, or a tax collector, their presence or absence is of no more importance than in the case of a thousand head of game in the savannas or the forests.

Don Gabriel had tried punishing the man by a multa of fifty pesos. He would gladly have settled for these fifty pesos, but the Indian did not have them. He could not have produced them even if don Gabriel had been willing to wait a whole year adding another fifty pesos as interest of course. Don Gabriel had even tried this, but the man could not produce a surety. No one would stand surety for him, because it was likely that the man would be killed by a relation of the murdered man in revenge, and then the surety would be called upon.

If one Indian kills another, the whole village knows the cause of the murder. The motives are understood in all their bearings, in their whole moral and traditional aspect and origin. If the murder is considered to have been justified and inevitable on these grounds, neither the brother, the father, nor the son of the murdered man will avenge the murder. The verdict is that the victim brought it on himself by his own act and had had his deserts. It may happen, however, that a member of the family group, to whom perhaps the circumstances are better known, may not endorse the verdict of the village. He will then nurse his revenge and carry it out as soon as a drunken brawl or a dispute at a festival gives him the chance.

If the general opinion of the village is that the murder was without justification, the murderer himself knows this without needing to be told, as soon as his fit of rage or drunkenness is over. He then leaves the place of his own accord, taking his family with him. No one hinders him. If, however, he does not go, but lives on in the place as though nothing has occurred, he will be found dead in the bush or on his land before the next moon.

When opinion in the village is divided, one family group urging that the murder was without justification, another urging that the perpetrator had good cause, or was out of his mind with drink, or acted hastily and has since repented, then the chief advises him to leave the village and settle at a distance in the jungle. If he follows this advice all the families of the place will be reconciled with him.

It would have been simple to hand the murderer over to the casique of the place, but don Gabriel was in a position which made this impossible. He had been called upon by the village to put the murderer in prison for the safety of the place, as he was so drunk he threatened to kill anyone who came near him. If the secretary were now simply to hand him over he would be prejudicing his authority—and he needed all his authority as a source of profit. He might even create the impression that he was afraid of the murderer or his family, and he could not afford to show fear if he wanted to remain there as secretary and extort arbitrary taxes and fines from the inhabitants.

It would have been unwise to punish the man with a fine of ten pesos, a sum which he might somehow have been able to raise. Don Gabriel had already released a man charged with a far less serious offense for a fine of twelve pesos. Besides, a ten-peso multa might encourage robbers to attack and murder traders or travelers in the belief that ten pesos to the secretary would settle the matter, while they would profit by the hundred pesos which the trader had on him. The reasonings of uncivilized Indians, as of most uncivilized people, are often very odd; but they start from some perfectly rational assumption.

Don Gabriel did what judges and police officials do in other countries, too, when they do not exactly know how to deal with a prisoner. He let the man remain quietly in prison without telling him what he intended to do with him, hoping that something might arise which would give him his decision ready-made.

5

  The prisoner's keep cost neither don Gabriel nor the State anything. The prisoner's wife had to prepare his meals and bring them to him, and if he had had no wife, then his mother or his brothers or some relation or other would have had to provide for him.

With a patience which never flagged or wearied or allowed a word of reproach to escape, his wife came three times a day to the prison with her children to feed her husband, give him clean clothes and tobacco, and see to all his needs.

Sometimes, if don Gabriel was in the mood to let him out, the whole family sat outside the prison door and ate their meal together. If any of his friends had the time or the wish, they came and squatted outside the prison and talked to him. Most nights his wife slept with her baby on a mat just outside the prison door so as to be near her husband. She did all that had to be done in his fields and for his animals, and if her strength or time gave out her brothers came and helped her.

During this time Narciso had been to the cabildo several times to discuss official business with don Gabriel, but on these occasions the prisoner's name had never been mentioned. Then one day when don Gabriel was alone, his brother Mateo having gone hunting in the jungle, Narciso sat down on the bench in the office and said, "Don Gabriel, what are you going to do now with Gregorio, who killed Aurelio? Are you going to keep him all his life here in jail?"

Don Gabriel uncorked the ink bottle, smelled the ink, corked it up again, and said, "You are presidente here and are acquainted with the laws and regulations."

"Certainly I know them," answered Narciso.

"Then you must know," don Gabriel went on, "that murder is a very serious and a very terrible thing. Gregorio will be shot."

"Yes, I know that," answered Narciso.

"If he could pay a hundred pesos or at least fifty pesos multa," said don Gabriel, "then I could let him go free."

"Gregorio has nothing like that," said Narciso, "and never will have in his whole life."

"I have been waiting till now, Narciso, for Gregorio's sake, and I have not yet telephoned to the municipalidad. But I cannot wait any longer. We must do something. Murder is a very serious matter. If I telephone, the soldiers will come and shoot him on the spot."

"Yes," said the jefe, "they undoubtedly will."

"But all the same I cannot let him go," don Gabriel continued. "I have no right to do that. Any ruffian here might think that he would get off as lightly. The consequences might be unpleasant. We might have a murder a week."

"It might be so," the jefe replied.

In the course of this discussion don Gabriel had an idea which so far had not occurred to him. Ever since he had taken up his position in the place he had never had an opportunity of going to Jovel to see how the world was getting along and whether any crevice had opened through which he might creep into a better crib. Now he might use Gregorio as an excuse for going to Jovel and be paid a daily allowance in addition. He had only to take Gregorio as a prisoner to the authorities, an official activity for which he would receive extra pay. It would be cheaper for the authorities if he took the man himself than if soldiers were sent either to carry out the sentence or to take him to the town to be sentenced there.

No sooner had this idea come into his head than he set about putting it into execution. "We have no right to pass sentence here in such a serious matter," he said, "neither you as presidente nor I as secretario. It is a matter for the courts. I must take him to Jovel and hand him over to the authorities there. I can tell you, Narciso, that this will be far better for him. The judges in Jovel will perhaps not be so hard upon him. They will condemn him to maybe three or four years in prison or in a labor colony, and when his time is up he will be set free, and then he can come back here to his own people. On the other hand, if the soldiers come here he will have little to hope for. They will either shoot him on the spot or else on their way back. They will say he attempted to escape, whether he did or not. They only have to invoke the Ley Fuga."

"I believe you are right, don Gabriel," the jefe said to this. "It will be best for him and it will give a good example to our ruffians here."

"Then I will go tomorrow, Narciso," said don Gabriel. "Don Mateo will take my place here as secretario. You agree to it?"

"Yes, I agree," replied Narciso. "I will go to his family and tell them that Gregorio will be taken tomorrow to the town to be tried."

As it was their own jefe who told them that it would be best for Gregorio to be taken to the town and tried there, his family and everybody else agreed. They knew quite well that there was nothing else to be done. Once there was a secretary representing the government in the place they had no right to settle this matter among themselves.

The prisoner's wife informed her husband that he would

be taken out next morning. Narciso went to him too, to tell him that he had to go quietly with don Gabriel to Jovel because that would be the best thing for him.

Gregorio took it, as far as could be seen, as unconcernedly as if he had been told that he was free to go home. His wife brought him his supper and sat outside the prison with her children till midnight, sometimes asleep, sometimes awake. She spoke a word or two to her husband now and then and kept the fire alight.

Soon after midnight she was back in her hut to cook him his breakfast and to prepare his provisions for the journey with the help of some neighbors, for it was a journey of four days or so.

Next morning at sunrise don Gabriel and his wife were ready to start. He was on horseback; his wife rode an old but surefooted mule. A second mule carried their packs for the journey. Gregorio had helped to get the animals ready for the road. He had been taken out of prison before sunrise to make himself useful. He was to act as their boy on the journey.

He went to his hut to pick up his provisions. He went unguarded and remained away an hour. If he had wished he could easily have made his escape, as he could do even more easily on the journey.

2

But Gregorio came back to the cabildo. It had been his destiny to kill Aurelio, and just as he had been able to do nothing against it so he could do nothing to interfere with the further course of his destiny in being sent to his trial in the town. What help would it have been to him to run away if that was not the decree of destiny? He might have escaped from don Gabriel and the soldiers and his judges, but he could never have outrun his fate.

And even if he had not felt himself to be a helpless pawn,

where would he have fled? If he had gone to the village of another tribe where his language was not spoken, he would have been a stranger there. Even if he settled down there, he would not have been taken into the community and no one would have accepted him. Their distrust of him would have increased every day. It would have been his fault that children died in infancy, that the maize did not flourish, that the sheep did not bear, that the stream changed its bed. Then one day his hut would have been burned down and his maize patch trodden underfoot. If he had stayed on in spite of this, one day he and his family would have been murdered.

He might have taken his wife and his children and settled in the jungle. But his feeling for community was so strong that he would not have been able to live for long in the jungle. He would have withered and pined without his family group. Sooner or later he would have had to return to his people. And if his tribe would then have condemned him to death it would have set his soul at rest and he would again have been in harmony with this world and thankful from the bottom of his heart that he could die among his own people. He might have survived in the jungle as an animal, but only in communion with his tribe could he live as a being conscious of human kinship.

He might have fled far away to a town where no one would have known him or bothered about him. But on the way he would have met people who would have asked him, "Where are you going, my friend, and why?" He could lie in the ordinary matters of his daily life, but it would have been beyond him to lie adroitly over complicated things and in strange surroundings and to strange people who looked distrustfully at him. He would have lost confidence and only aroused graver distrust, and at the next place been arrested by the authorities.

Or he might have crept cunningly by bush paths, avoiding anyone who was not an Indian, sleeping in the bush away from any path, and in that way reached the town. But everything would have been strange to him. He would have been unable to speak a word of Spanish, and besides the speech, the habits and way of life of the people would have made it impossible for him to find work that he could do. He would not even have known how to beg, nor how, when a man had no work, he could scrape out a living in a town. He would have found no plants or fruit growing in the town with which he could have satisfied his hunger as he could in the jungle or the bush. It might have been possible to find work helping ox-cart or mule drivers, but he would not have known how to approach them, and even such people would have been distrustful and sullen when not understanding a word he said.

Even if he had somehow had the luck to find work somewhere, it would have been the hardest, harshest, dirtiest, most wretched work, and he would have had to be on hand twenty-four hours a day for nothing but a starvation ration as wages. A laborer who asks for no wage is welcome even in Mexico. If he takes nothing else for his work than a plate of beans, which he receives with a grateful nod to his master, he is well liked and considered very polite.

Yet even such a refuge would not have been a rescue. The longing for his wife and children would one day have become so strong that he would have had to go back to them, without caring what happened to him. He would have been unable to live in separation from his family.

And so whatever he might have done he was in a trap from which there was no escape.

3

Gregorio took up his pack and set off on his journey.

His wife had gone far along the trail so as to take leave of him where the path entered the bush. She crouched there with her baby at her breast waiting for her husband. The other children scrambled about her.

The woman squatted on the ground, Indian fashion, weeping silently to herself, while she swayed the upper part of her body to and fro in a rhythm which no doubt kept time with the painful throb of her emotions. She clutched her infant to her heart and then released it in the same rhythm. It was as though all her pain was inspired only by the little child. It drew forth the physical emotion she would not and perhaps could not show for her husband.

The relation of an Indian to his wife and of an Indian woman to her husband is as close as any love can be. Yet its expression is crude—so crude that a European is profoundly affected by its crudity, because, since the inexpressible feelings of the heart are the same in all human beings and are felt in the same way, this very crudity only deepens the impression made by the strength of their feelings. The strength of their feelings is so deep, so genuine—because it is so primitive—so violent and so true that they lack all power to dissemble them. It is because they cannot endure that the least trace of dissembling should creep into the expression of their feelings that they give them this outward appearance of crudity. It is not a mask to hide their true feelings; it is merely a spontaneous protection against the outbreak of overwhelming and violent emotion. If they did not put a strong curb on their feelings they might be led to an exposure of their deepest emotions; their neighbors would laugh at them, their innermost feelings would be cheapened, and they would never get over the pang of shame at having lost the modesty which is like a bloom on their feelings, however old they may be.

Gregorio came along with a rolling step, bent double under the weight of his pack. He did not look up; owing to the strap of his pack which pressed on his forehead he could see only a step or two in front of him and could glance only a little way to right or left. So he did not see that his wife was there.

When he was only three steps from her he gave a jerk to his load to make it sit better, and then he saw his wife crouching beside the path.

"Huj!" he blurted out.

He was surprised to see her there. He stopped, but turned only halfway toward her, as though to show that he had no intention of halting, still less of resting.

The woman held up her child for her husband to see. Her breast was bare. Noticing this she caught her dress together, but in her haste and excitement she did not pause to fasten it.

Raising herself a little she got up on her knees, still holding the child out to her husband. Then she began to cry aloud like an animal. Her face, which was unwashed and swollen with nights of weeping, seemed to be blotted out but for her wide-open purple mouth and powerful teeth. Her two black eyes were thin streaks from which her tears poured. Her thick black hair was tousled and unkempt; its matted strands were like the tangled branches of a dense bush of the jungle. Her short broad nose was distended, and its wide nostrils looked like the cavernous openings to an unknown world behind the weathered and copper-colored face.

In long-drawn sobs she uttered the wailing cries of an Indian woman who feels the ruthlessness of the world about her, and the wretchedness of being harnessed to it by physical needs and feelings which make the lot of a dumb animal enviable in comparison; for the animal is spared at least all feeling for the future.

It was her lamentation over a dead child, her dead mother, her dead husband. She did not need to be told—she knew that her husband was being taken from her never to return, just as a sheep, driven from the village by a dealer, never returned. He was an animal, though he could talk and laugh—without a soul, according to the views of those who were to sit in judgment on him. Dirty, lousy, baptized a Catholic and yet a heathen, as untaught as a dog, greedy for brandy, with his work-hardened hands like ebony, and the hair on his head worn by the untanned thongs which harnessed him to many loads, worn and bare like the rubbed places on the flanks of a pack mule—a victim to be butchered at the will of those who had conquered his land and his race.

The woman knew as little of all that went to make up her destiny as her husband did. A cow driven by dealers to the butcher does not look for a chance to escape on the way there, and just as little did she think that her husband could ever return. She knew how cattle were driven off; and as she knew from a hundred instances that the great patroncitos, the gentry with revolvers in their belts, made no distinction between cattle and Indians, she knew also that she saw her husband for the last time.

No thought for what would come of herself and her children was concealed in her piercing cries. That did not touch her. The children had been born and they would eat and live. The morning was far off, and when it came the table would be spread.

She was wrought up to this volcanic pitch of grief only by her husband's fate; and her suffering was not provoked by the thought of him as her bedfellow or the provider for her children. That was nothing. It would not have provoked her to cry out, scarcely even to whimper.

But her husband was the father of her children, who were like the beat of her own heart. The altar at which her children prayed was in ruins. And for her, his wife, the central point of her life was in ruins. Her husband might be a drunkard; he might beat her and work her to the bone; but all the same he was the core of her being. All her thoughts and acts and cares were centered in him; he was her religion, her master, her only friend and dearest comrade. He was her real home and all she knew as country. He was the life of the world about her, and without him it fell to pieces. It was not the problems of existence that bound her to him. These could be solved with the help of her clan, harshly perhaps, but with tolerable certainty. It was her soul that was empty and meaningless without him, just as the souls of people who have no personal feelings are empty when their God or their idols or saints are taken from them.

Her grief was not for herself; she had no pity for herself. The grief that shook her was the expression of her pain, the almost physical pain of being torn asunder, of having a piece of her very self, the greater part, indeed, of her being, cut from her.

4

The children heard her cries and came up and crowded about her and began to cry when they saw the sorrow she was in.

Gregorio at first had stopped and looked at her as though she were no longer a part of him and he had meant to go on again. But at the sight of her despair, and even more perhaps at the sight of the naked struggling infant which she held up to him, he went to her and knelt down and took the thong from his forehead.

"Tata, Tata," cried the children, scrambling about him. They stopped crying as soon as they saw that their mother was calmer for a moment with her husband at her side.

He could stay only a few minutes, but these fleeting minutes which she lived with every sense and feeling were the experience of a hundred years. She did not rob them of one second by wasting a single thought on the future. Not one of these minutes would ever come again; what was not felt and lived then, eternities could not make good.

Gregorio's face showed nothing of what went on inside him.

He took the baby from his wife's outstretched arms and nursed it on his knees; he caressed his own face softly with its round brown cheeks.

His lips moved as though parched, but he did not utter a word—not a word of comfort, not one of vain hope of a return. It was his fate to be as the beasts. He had no power or chance of influencing this fate. Neither his yes nor his no could influence it at all. He had to accept what the patroncitos decided and what they would do with him. Human kindness and mutual understanding dwell far outside the limits of the world, and the all-wise and all-just Creator of all things remains invisible and inscrutable, so that His priests may not lose the profits of the vineyard.

The woman sobbed gently and edged nearer to her husband to feel him. Now and again she said "Gregorio, Gregorio." They were the only words into which she could put the feelings that went through her.

He gave her no instructions on what she was to do when he had gone, nor did she ask for any. There would be time to see to all that when it arose.

The children had begun to play about again. The man and the woman sat quietly together without looking at each other. Both looked straight in front of them at the narrow path, as if they were trying to judge how recent were the half-obliterated hoofprints of the horses and mules which had passed that way.

It is certain that neither of them thought of anything, that the world around them vanished and that they had lost all sense of conscious existence, as though they were in a deep sleep. But suddenly they were harshly and mercilessly wrenched back to reality.

"Oye, listen you Gregorio, get on, get on!"

It was don Gabriel riding up with his wife. His wife rode first, the pack mule followed, and behind them came don Gabriel. As soon as he had seen Gregorio sitting there he had felt that he ought to say something to show his authority, although he knew that the Indian, in spite of his heavy pack, could not only keep pace with the animals, but would generally be far ahead. He could climb up steep hills and make his way straight across ravines where the animals could not go. He would take the shortest way, while the animals sometimes would have to make long detours.

" 'Orita, señor," answered Gregorio. "Ya me voy, I'm coming right now."

He got up as he spoke and gave the baby back to his wife. Don Gabriel, without slackening his pace, rode heedlessly on.

The woman clutched the little one desperately to her with feverish movements of her arms and hands. As she could not embrace her husband and press him to her, because that was not their custom, and yet was compelled to give some physical expression to what she felt at that moment, she overwhelmed her child with the caresses which in her heart she meant for him.

She remained squatting where she was. With her lips tightly closed she looked up at her husband with large moist eyes and followed every movement he made as he got ready to go, as though she wanted to learn each by heart. She shook her head vigorously several times as though saying no to something which could never be.

While she watched her husband she over and over again caught hold of one of the baby's hands and, grasping it spasmodically between her fingers, put it into her mouth, gently biting and sucking at it, entirely unconscious of what she did.

When Gregorio had got his pack together, he bent down to put the strap against his head and then, with a short, springy jerk forward, stood up. Now he turned to his wife with his load on his back. He gave her his hand and she, after the manner of her race, touched the first joints of the fingers without pressing his hand. But before their hands separated she held his hand fast and kissed it.

His face was sad and a shadow passed over it. He half closed his eyes, swallowed hard, and pulled with his left hand at the thong over his forehead to settle it more comfortably. For the fraction of a second he pressed his hand to his wife's lips and then pulled it quickly away.

His wife held up the infant and he put his fingertips on its head. Raising her voice the woman called out, "Muchachos, Tata is going."

The children gathered around and each, even the youngest, took his father's hand and kissed it. In reply he touched each child on the head. Then the children ran off again.

He stood in front of his wife for a moment. He looked down at her in her unwashed and tear-stained misery, her every muscle and sinew taut and cramped in the wild effort to resist the tumult of emotion by which she was torn and which now began at last to get the upper hand. Her baby hung at her naked breast. Her swimming eyes, from which long round drops overflowed, were fixed upon him, and her naked legs and bare, calloused feet projected from the black tattered woolen smock which was all she had. He looked at her and saw in her, as never before, the whole meaning of his home and his world. He saw this world rise before him for the first time in his existence, and as it rose it fell apart. He opened his mouth to draw a deep breath, but before he could do so he pressed his lips tightly together again.

Then he turned quickly and went his way without saying a word, without looking back, without pausing. He had not taken ten steps before the bush closed behind him.

6

 Two days later don Gabriel, with his wife and Gregorio, reached the large Indian town of Cahancu late in the afternoon.

The town was an important stage for all pack-mule trains coming from the southern and central districts of the state. The roads leading north, northeast, and northwest branched off here, and so it was an important market. The caravans bought what they needed for the rest of their journey, whether provisions or new bits of pack-saddle harness to replace those that had given out. Often the caravans spent a whole day to give the animals a good rest before embarking on the bad roads ahead of them, or to redistribute the loads according to the capacity and endurance which each mule had shown. The saddle sores of the animals, caused partly by the rubbing of badly balanced loads and partly by the fierce bites of large insects, were thoroughly doctored. If this was not done, these wounds, before many stages were over, would have been full of finger-long worms, which in a few days would have penetrated beneath the hide and begun to devour the animal alive until it finally collapsed and died by the road.

Cahancu was situated on a high, flat-topped hill, which was

entirely occupied by the plaza. The Indians lived all around on the sides of the hill and below were their fields and cultivated land. No Indians lived on the plaza. Only Ladinos lived there.

The plaza was in the shape of a large rectangle. One end was bounded by the church, the other by the cabildo, where the secretary of the place lived and exercised his authority. As in all places with an Indian population, the head of their community was an Indian, who lived among his people.

One of the long sides of the rectangle was occupied by a rambling colonial building with a colonnade along its whole length. Here were the fondas, or inns, where travelers passing through could eat. They contained a few windowless rooms with bare bedsteads. Leather thongs were stretched along and across and securely fastened to the bedsteads. A straw mat was laid over this network of thongs, which still had hair on them, as they had never been tanned. The bedsteads in these rooms were let to travelers. There were four or eight of them to each room without so much as a curtain or a movable screen between them.

It was chiefly women travelers who took beds. Very little was charged for them, usually nothing at all. They were thrown in with the supper, which was cheap, whether you slept on one of the beds or not.

With very few exceptions men slept along the open colonnade, where they hung their hammocks or lay on the mud floor with a mat under them, and covered by a blanket and a mosquito net. Often enough women, too, slept without concern along the colonnade, particularly when they were traveling with their husbands, for it was usually cooler there than in the stuffy rooms.

This colonnade, although extensive, was often so full of packs, saddles, and sleepers that there was scarcely room to walk. Sometimes there were as many as ten hammocks with a man or a woman sleeping in each and mule drivers and passive Indians sleeping on the ground beneath them. It was never quiet during the night in this colonnade, nor in the plaza as a whole did the chattering and haggling and babbling of half-drunken mule drivers and Indians ever cease.

Caravans or travelers kept arriving at all hours throughout the night, or else parties were starting off, particularly when there was a moon. The fires of the Indians and the mule drivers burned all night long outside the colonnade, and here they cooked their food, because even the low charges at the inns were more than they could pay. All night long people packed, talked, quarreled, cursed, smoked, and discussed the next day's stage.

The kitchens were at the end of the colonnade nearest the cabildo. Here too there was cooking and talking all the night through. Before the last supper had been served up for a traveler who had just come in, people were already waiting for their breakfasts, ready to start off.

All races and callings were to be found in this colonnade—American engineers, Swedish geologists, Arabian traders, Spanish commercial travelers, Mexican archaeologists, Negroes, Polish Jews, Chinese opium smugglers, Indian porters, escaped convicts and murderers—but whatever had brought them here, they were all peaceable and friendly. If anyone had his head accidentally trodden on during the night by someone in a hurry to be off, or got a hefty kick in the ribs which left a bruise, he cursed for a moment, upon which the man who had done it excused himself politely and volubly. Then the sufferer, rubbing the injured part, replied even more politely, "Nothing at all, señor, always at your service." Peace and harmony were not disturbed by accidents like that, for everyone knew that no one had the intention of annoying anybody else.

The other long side of the plaza was occupied by shops. These houses of business were thatched huts and wooden shacks. Each looked as if it would fall to pieces at any moment, as it certainly would have had it not been held up by its neighbor, which also waited in an equally sorry state for the next puff of wind in order to take its final leave of a cruel world. But although these shops consisted only of boards, laths, sticks, rags, bundles of straw, palm leaves, cardboard, scraps of tin, bits of wire, empty gasoline and paraffin cans, hides, mats, and remnants of broken packing cases, they nevertheless looked as though they had been standing there when Noah was told to build an ark.

Each offered for sale very much the same articles as its neighbor. Many shops contained only three pesos' worth of goods in all, but the occupants appeared to make a living by them. The shopkeepers were mostly women. Nobody knew, not even the women themselves, where their husbands were to be found, and they could seldom say how they came to lose them. Every one of them, however, had a number of children as a perpetual reminder that she once had one husband at least.

These shops were by no means enclosed structures. Properly seen, they were only boards laid over boxes or blocks of old wood to form a counter. Behind the counter there were sometimes roughly made shelves onto which goods were crammed and thrown together without order or method, to wait there ten years or more for purchasers.

The counter and the shelves were roofed over in every possible way that ingenuity could devise. To the left and right of the counter were partitions to show where one shop ended and the next began.

Hanging from the crazy roofs was every article which could possibly be asked for: rope, belts, candles, coffeepots, lanterns, mule-drivers' whips, spurs, sandals, women's patent-leather shoes, bags of bast and leather, shotguns, tinderboxes containing flint, steel and tinder; images of the saints, large bright-red neckerchiefs, gigantic straw hats, machetes, cotton shirts, and party dresses.

There were scales on the counter, placed in such a way that the purchaser could never ascertain whether they weighed correctly or not. In most cases the saleswoman was not able to tell. But scales were obligatory and so they were there.

There were bottles of beer, soda water, and lemonade on the counter, and bananas, oranges, lemons, pastries, cocoa beans, pumpkin seeds. There were enticing pieces of candy in jars and bottles.

At night the shops were lit up. Each had a different lighting system. The large and up-to-date shops burned kerosene, acetylene, oil, or gasoline. The smaller shops used candles, and the smallest pine splinters.

In front of the shops was a row of Indian food stalls which had neither roofs nor tables nor chairs. Anyone who wanted a meal crouched on the ground or stood as he ate. The customers were mostly wandering Indians or caravan drivers too tired to cook for themselves. These open-air kitchens were kept going all through the night. The Indian cooks squatted beside their little tin stoves and slept; but as soon as anyone stopped in front of them the women were alive all at once, and without the guest's needing to say a word the fire was fanned and a few dry tortillas were thrown into the shallow pan over the fire to be warmed up or fried. Coffee was always ready, for the pot stood close by the fire.

The shops could not be locked up and it would have been useless to have locked them, since no more than a touch of a foot would have been needed to break into them. A lock would have been mere ostentation.

But as with the little Indian food stalls, so too in the case of the shops there was no closing time. You could shop there all night through. You needed only to summon the woman.

When the tide of business began to ebb at about ten o'clock

and only the brandy shops were still busy, because the mule drivers were there for their nightcaps, the shopwomen cleared their counters. Everything was packed away underneath or stuffed into any corner or box where there was room for it.

In some of the shops boards were stood on the counter in such a way that they leaned against the thatch. This was to show that the shop was shut and that you could get what you wanted only by going to the back or side door. This back or side door was composed during the day of a fragment of sacking and during the night of two or three propped-up rotten planks.

As soon as the counter was cleared, so that no one prowling about in the dark of the night could lay hands on anything, the shopwoman, with the help of her children and maids, put together somewhere in this tiny building a medley of things impossible to distinguish or describe, but the woman called it, nonetheless, la cama, the bed. She took the smallest child into bed with her. The older children slept on the counter to protect the establishment from robbery and theft. The other children were rolled into blankets and put on boxes, sacks, mats, boards, or torn mattresses; and the maids—there were often two or three of them—were content to creep into any corner as long as they could sleep inside the house. Sometimes they too had children, an infant at the breast or a larger child.

At last the mosquito nets were spread and the whole shop sank to rest in preparation for the heavy labor of the coming day.

The space between the counter and the rickety back wall that separated the shop from the bush behind it served not only as a storehouse and bedroom, but also as kitchen and dining room, and as reception room for the noisy occasions when the women celebrated their saints' days.

These shops, wretched, sordid, primitive, and yet busy all the same, filled an important role in the town—not, as you might think, because they supplied travelers and caravans with all the indispensable articles required on their long and difficult journeys. That was only incidental. Their most important function was to swell the profits of the secretary of the place. Every shop, however small and unassuming, and every tiny open-air kitchen that sold tortillas and beans, and every Indian who set out bananas and oranges on the ground to sell to passing mule drivers had taxes to pay; and the taxes were paid to the secretary.

The secretary had to account for these taxes to the government of the state. The accounts were extremely complicated and more than ordinarily voluminous owing to the many small and very small businesses. Some of them were so small they were assessed at only two centavos a day. These were the wares of the Indian who spread out on the ground the beans, onions, or chiles they had grown themselves, and squatted behind them and waited for someone to come along who thought that here was an Indian with something to give away. The only man on earth who could give the state any account of the taxability of the place and of the source and method of taxation was the secretary. As he was no student of political economy nobody expected him to be very clear on the matter. And as the revenue officials were still less at home in this maze, all the less because of their advanced mathematics, and as in the last resort only the secretary of the place could decide what the tax should be for each single business according to its profits, and as no mathematician could hope to check or analyze this medley of deductions and rebates and surcharges and special taxes and brandy license fees which the secretary fixed to suit his own advantage, the post of secretary in this lively place of call was an extremely enviable one.

In addition to the taxes there were fines for which the secretary gave receipts or not as he chose. He also ordained what offenses were subject to fines. There was no arguing the matter. He was in authority. He had a revolver and four Indian policemen with shotguns and machetes.

2

When don Gabriel arrived he rode straight to the cabildo to pay his respects to the secretary. He intended to spend the night in the cabildo, since he would thus have an opportunity of discussing official questions with the secretary. Such conferences between two secretaries who happen to meet are always concerned with the measures one or the other has found of use in adding to his profits. In this they closely resemble the confabulations between saviors of souls who also meet sometimes on each other's beats. Their object, too, is to discuss the best means of exploiting every opportunity for gain which their office affords rather than to consider the spiritual welfare of their flocks.

As in all places of this description the secretary offered food and shelter to boarders of the better sort in return for the usual payment. This right to keep a hotel was one of his perquisites and it was the only business in the town on which no tax was paid. Autocracy is always tax-free. The secretary with his hostelry was naturally more than able to compete with the other fondas, which carried on business in the long colonial building on the plaza; for travelers who could pay well never patronized these places unless the secretary was so full up that he could not take them. He made a profit not only on the meals supplied to the travelers, but also by supplying fodder for their horses and mules, as well as by providing for the travelers' servants.

Besides all this, he kept a bar which was well patronized by all travelers who boarded with him; and this meant the loss of much trade to other bars in the town, which had to pay a large sum for the license to sell brandy.

Not satisfied with this, he ran a tienda in the cabildo and

offered for sale all the articles from which the women in the shops endeavored to make a living for themselves and their families.

It must be mentioned, however, that he never used his position and influence in order to discriminate officially in favor of travelers who lodged with him or dealt with him. That was one reason why the tradespeople of the town put up with his unfair competition instead of complaining of it to the government.

In any case, a complaint would have done them more harm than good. The complainants would have had to give their names. The secretary would have found out who they were and taken it out on them to such an extent that they would have bitterly rued the day for years to come.

All the same, there were people who had the courage to make complaints, but they were to be found rather among those whose indignation over the injustice and arbitrary doings of the secretary made them indifferent to their own fate.

Hence there was deadly enmity between the secretary and the Ladinos of the place. It was not an open enmity. Face to face there was a show of mutual toleration. But behind there was hatred unrelieved.

3

Don Rafael Sariol, the secretary of the place, was not at home when don Gabriel and his wife reached the cabildo. The secretary's wife received the new arrivals. She welcomed don Gabriel's wife with great kindness, for she knew from her own experience what so long a journey on a mule over such unspeakably bad roads meant for a woman.

Even though Mexican women who live on remote ranches and haciendas are as tough on a long journey as any hardboiled robber baron of the Teutonic middle ages, and even though they can toss down a full-sized glass of strong tequila at one go without batting an eyelash, all the same these long treks on a mule or horse which is always starting or stumbling or coming down on its knees are nothing but martyrdom. They are torture for a man, and worse for a woman—let alone for women who have given birth to several children on remote farms with no help but that which some old Indian woman could give them.

The roads are so bad that even a knowing old mule cannot go at an even pace, however much it may want to. Trunks of huge trees, torn down by the last hurricane or the last but one, lie across the trail, their diameters a yard or a yard and a half across. The mule has to jump them whether it likes or not. Next it sinks into deep holes and pits washed out by the rain, or gets a foot caught between the exposed roots of trees. Then comes a steep descent and the beast clambers down with its hindquarters nearly perpendicular to its head. Then it has to leap a wide chasm and lands with its forefeet only, its hind legs hanging over the void. Its rider does not know for a few exciting seconds whether the animal will make it with its hind feet or whether it will fall back into the cleft and land fifty feet below with the rider beneath. So it goes on, varied only by even more hair-raising obstacles—and goes on for six days or seven or twelve.

Each day starts at six and ends at four or five. It would not be so bad if the woman could sit in the most comfortable way for so long and exhausting a journey. But convention does not permit any deviation from the seat enjoined upon the Mexican woman. She may not use a man's saddle and still less sit astride. The saddle she uses for these long and exacting journeys through bush, jungle, and morass is exactly the same as those the noble ladies of Spain used when they rode out hunting in the days when Charles V first heard that by the conquest of Mexico a new province had been added to his realm. How could she possibly ride in any other manner? What would the world think and say if she was encountered by the wives of reputable rancheros, sitting on a mule like any slovenly disreputable Protestant gringa, who believes neither in the saints nor the Immaculate Conception? And what would the cura say if he saw it or heard of it? There is no propriety without discomfort.

And since don Gabriel's wife arrived riding in a reputable and well-bred manner, don Rafael's wife knew that no attentions could be too many to make up for the sufferings she must have gone through.

When they sat down later to a meal, don Gabriel's wife explained what it was that had brought her husband from home; and as there was no one else present she could, as she made a point of saying at the outset, speak freely. Don Gabriel too was a secretario and so it was a family matter.

4

On the open space near the church where a narrow path led down to the Indian settlement an armorer had set up his workshop. He was a mestizo.

The armorer's shop was open on all sides and consisted merely of six posts driven into the ground to support a roof of palm leaves. Beneath this canopy was a small field forge. There was also a diminutive anvil, which was perhaps large enough to do for a watchmaker; and a small vise was attached to a tree trunk which was rotting in the earth.

This was the armorer's smithy. There was nothing to show whether the man to whom this armament firm belonged was really an armorer. He might just as well have been a tanner or a furrier. But nobody asked him for his credentials. A crow can pass for a peacock or a nightingale when there is no rivalry and nobody knows the difference. And as the next armorer was twenty kilometers away and as he too was an armorer only because rope-making did not pay, this one here had plenty of work. Every Indian whose muzzle-loader had gone wrong and shot backward had to come to him. He put new barrels on, fitted new hammers, put new springs in the lock, hammered the triggers into shape, and bored out choked and rusted nipples. He did not overwork himself. He took his time. He was well up to spending half a day on a job that he could easily have done in five minutes.

The Indian sat patiently looking on and waited as patiently when the smith interrupted his work to go for a meal and spent two hours over it. The longer the job took him the more difficult it seemed to the Indian and the more willing he was to pay a round peso for a job for which a thank you or ten centavos would have been quite enough.

The whole day long there was always a group of Indians squatting near the smithy to watch the man at his impressive labors. A firearm, even if it is only a muzzle-loader, is an important matter in the lives of these Indians. And a man who understands how to cure the ills of a shotgun is a man of mark, whose work calls for admiration.

Two traders who were both on a journey and spending the night in the place got into an argument in front of the armorer's shop. The point of dispute was the best bore for shooting jaguars and mountain lions. Three bores came into question—twelve, sixteen, and twenty. Unless there had been a fixed intention to embark on a heated argument and unless some previous encounter at a market somewhere had left enmity behind it, it would have been easy enough to reconcile such a difference of opinion by agreeing straightway that you could shoot jaguar with any bore as long as you shot straight; for if you don't it makes no difference if you shoot at the jaguar with a twelve-inch shell.

One of these traders, don Ismael, was an Arabian; the other, don Martín, was a Mexican. The two were always quarreling whenever they met. Each accused the other of spoiling his business and reducing him to starvation by undercutting his prices, and of shouting out "Here, señorita, I can sell you genuine French stockings, imported only yesterday, for two reales cheaper" as soon as the other had a woman at his stall who was ready to buy silk stockings and had the money in her hand. It was shabby behavior, and it was practiced by each merely to put the other in a rage.

Now the two had met again, don Martín on his way down from Montecristo and don Ismael from Tuxtla on his way to Tumbalá.

The question of the right bore for a jaguar was only the prelude. Very soon don Ismael was saying that Mexicans were so stupid they did not even know the difference between a machine gun and a howitzer. Neither of them knew what a howitzer was—don Ismael had picked up the word somewhere—but don Martín was nonetheless insulted. He replied the Arabians were such barbarous heathen that they were not ashamed to sleep in the straw with pigs, camels, donkeys, children, and ten wives.

To this don Ismael answered that don Martín owed his existence only to the fact that his mother, when she bore a litter of half a dozen puppies, had by an oversight missed drowning one of them, and the very one which was afflicted with festering boils because his father was eaten up with a certain disease which he need not specify. What don Martín said to this cannot be put into such plain and harmless words, but it was as fantastic as only such remarks can be when a Mexican, particularly if he is a traveling merchant, means his opponent to whip out his revolver and empty all six chambers without further reflection.

Don Ismael, however, did not have his revolver in his belt. He had left it at his fonda, since he had only come out for a pleasant stroll. But he had a sheath knife stuck into his belt.

He had the knife out in a flash. Don Martín was as quick with his revolver, but it took him a moment longer to cock the trigger. Thus it was that he got a severe stab in his side before he could fire. The bullet rattled against the roof of the church, and before he could fire a second time don Ismael had knocked his arm down and, catching hold of his hand, twisted his wrist until the weapon fell to the ground.

Don Rafael, the secretary, was only about a hundred yards away, speaking to some mule drivers, while all this was going on. As soon as he heard the shot he came up at a run, just in time to prevent don Martín's recovering the revolver on which don Ismael had put his foot.

His four policemen also came running up at the sound of the shot. They were Indians, barefoot, without hats, machetes at their sides and old muzzle-loaders slung from their shoulders. As soon as they saw that the brawl was not between Indians they came to a stop a short way off.

Indian police in small places are very cautious in their dealings with people who are not of their race. If Mexicans or other caballeros choose to scrap or even open rapid fire on one another, they do not intervene unless directly ordered to do so by the secretary, for caballeros have their own way of amusing themselves. Besides, the disputants may be high officials, who can have a policeman locked up if he interferes in matters which do not concern him. It is another thing with Indians. An Indian policeman knows where he is with them and if they do not come quietly he gives them a good crack over the head with his wooden truncheon.

An Indian policeman knows also that the caballero does not run away, even when he has shot his opponent dead. The caballero has no reason to run away. The caballero is a brave man and always faces the consequences of his actions. He is well aware that he lives in Mexico, and that nothing can be done to him in a little place for a chance murder, and that he can always find a judge in the large towns who can be persuaded with astonishing ease that it was no murder at all, but a matter of self-defense or of wounded honor. The Indian does not get away with it so lightly once they lay hands on him. For this reason he tries to make himself scarce while he has a chance.

"Caballeros," don Rafael said in a friendly tone, "siento mucho, I'm really sorry, but I find myself compelled to arrest you both for disturbance of the peace. Accompany me, if you please, to the cabildo."

Don Martín felt a little weak owing to the knife wound in his side and so had to throw in his hand; and as don Ismael saw that he had no fight in him, he calmed down too. Both of them walked slowly to the cabildo with the secretary, followed by the Indian policemen.

Don Martín, the Mexican, was putting up at the cabildo and thus was the secretary's guest, while don Ismael, the Arab, was spending the night in one of the fondas off the colonnade.

"Pase, caballeros, come in," said don Rafael as he led his two prisoners into the large sala. This so-called living room was the secretary's office, but served equally as living room, dining room, and bedroom all in one for his paying guests. It was large enough for twenty people to pitch their camp in for the night, and sometimes it contained as many as thirty.

The two men sat down. The four policemen squatted in the open doorway in order, however involuntarily, to give the trial a proper tone.

Don Rafael brought out a full bottle of comiteco and they had two rounds before the judicial proceedings began. During the two rounds the three caballeros discussed the weather, the state of business, the price of horses, and acquaintances who had lately passed through.

Finally, don Martín said, "Oiga, señor Secretario—listen, do you think the señora Esposa, your wife, has any lint about? I suppose I ought to stop up this wound."

"Oh, so you're wounded, are you, don Martín?" said the secretary. "Let me have a look."

Don Martín loosened his belt, pulled up his shirt, which was soaked in blood, and showed the wound.

A European with a gash like that would hardly have been able to inspect it without thinking of his death, his last will and testament, the operating table—and then faint away. But a Mexican does not faint at such a triviality and still less does he think of death. He looks at his wound with a professional eye, compares it with all the other knife and shot wounds which he has already survived, and with those of others he has seen, prods it with his finger, and allows his boon companions to give their verdict on it and to prod it themselves, so that their verdict will proceed from firsthand evidence.

And so it was here. Each of the three computed how long it would take for the wound to heal, but not one of them thought of a doctor or a hospital, which would have been useless to consider in any case, because the nearest doctor was so far away that the wound would certainly have healed before the doctor could set eyes on it.

The secretary's wife brought some wadding and a bandage. The wound was washed, brandy was poured into it, and finally the wadding was stuffed in and the bandage applied. When all this was done to their satisfaction don Rafael said, "Now we must look into this business. It is my duty to take you both to the capital of the district to stand trial."

"What is there to have a trial about?" said don Martín. "It has nothing to do with the courts if this son of a whore stuck his knife into me. I've got it now, and if I don't choose to let this boil-stricken Turk tell me to my face that my mother is a ten-centavo whore, that doesn't concern the courts or any district capital. The gash is there and no judge can do away with it."

"But what about all he said to me, the mangy coyote?" don

Ismael asked. "I don't want any judge in the district capital, nor his bloody good advice. He'd tell me I ought to stand and look on while this scab swung his revolver and planted a half dozen forty-fives in my guts. A lot of good a judge'd be to me once I'd swallowed them and couldn't digest them."

Don Rafael did not bother with the two traders' private affairs, but when he thought that they had both got it off their chests and had no more reserves left in their rich vocabulary, he said, "I see, caballeros, that you don't fancy the notion of a judge, so we may as well settle the matter among ourselves. Justice we must have. You will agree with me there, señores. Don Ismael, you stabbed a man in this peaceable town and I must fine you a hundred and fifty pesos for assault and fifty pesos for disturbance of the peace. That comes to two hundred pesos, which you must pay now or else I shall have to put you under arrest until the multa is paid."

Don Ismael wanted to make an objection, but don Rafael said, "Un momento, this is an official matter."

He then turned to don Martín. "I must punish you, señor, with a multa of fifty pesos because you drew your revolver on another man in a peaceable place without just cause. And as you, like don Ismael, disturbed the public peace, I must fine you fifty pesos for that also. That comes to a hundred pesos, which you must pay now or else I must put you under arrest until the multa is discharged."

All three of them, the secretary as well as the two traders, knew that this was not the last word. Next came the appeal, which was immediately lodged by both. The judge of appeal was the same judge who had just given the verdict. This was a great simplification of the judicial proceedings and a great saving to the State.

The secretary had the right to put both men under arrest and if necessary to send them both under guard to the district capital; but he also had the right in urgent cases to settle the matter himself on the spot. It could not be denied that the case was urgent. The two traders were traveling on business. It would have damaged their business if they had had now to go to the district capital and wait there three or perhaps six weeks until the case came up. From every aspect it was cheaper and more convenient to get through all the stages of the judicial proceedings on the spot. As regards the fines, there was no hope that a regular judge would do it any cheaper than the secretary—and there would be the costs, which would be considerable, on top of the fines.

The secretary could have overlooked the whole episode, as he certainly would have done in the case of good friends of his or officials with political influence. But he had to live, and such an opportunity of pocketing a decent sum at one blow did not come every day.

Yet he was also a good enough diplomat not to make enemies for himself. It was unlikely he would be secretary there forever. One fine day his taxation accounts and his post office and telegraph accounts would be found to be not in order and then his palmy days would be over. It might then happen that he himself would be a trader, and the day might come when he needed don Ismael's help, or that don Martín was the secretary somewhere and could give him a break.

"I might let you off scot-free, caballeros," said he, "but it's more than I dare do. I am in an official position. It would make a very bad impression on the inhabitants, not least on the Indians, if I overlooked what has occurred. It might seriously compromise my authority. That wouldn't do. You can see that for yourselves. The world can only be ruled with justice and impartiality."

"That may all be quite correct," said don Martín to this, "but I don't have the money and I can't stay here in prison. I must get to the feria in good time or I'll get a bad stand."

"I'm in the same boat," said don Ismael. "I haven't a day to lose. I'm already half a week behind in my business without this, owing to the cursed state of the roads."

When at last the appeal, oiled by a few more glasses of comiteco, had been decided, it came out that don Martín had to pay twenty pesos and don Ismael fifty. Don Ismael could spare no cash because he needed it for business deals on the journey. Instead he gave the secretary a spare horse he had along, which he assured him was worth a hundred and twenty pesos.

Don Rafael was more set on hard coin than good horseflesh and lost no time in selling the horse. It was owing to his having gone to complete the sale that don Gabriel had not found him at home.

7

Don Gabriel, finding his wife engaged in a long talk with don Rafael's wife that did not interest him, strolled out to the plaza hoping to meet someone he could chat with.

Men get indignant about idle gossip only when it is a question of gossip between women; but when they themselves get together, they can beat half a dozen fishwives at the game. A man thinks his wearisome gabble is intelligent discussion of political and economic questions, and considers the chatter of women as senseless rubbish. But looked at impartially the rubbish talked by men is no better or richer in ideas than the rubbish talked by women. The topics are slightly different, but the aim and result are as alike as a Ford and a Dodge.

In the course of his stroll don Gabriel landed in the colonnade where the fondas were. He felt sure he would meet some dealer or muleteer there whom he knew and could pass the next few hours with.

There was not much going on that day in the colonnade. A few Indian porters squatted beside their loads smoking fat cigars while their beans cooked in a pot over the fire that burned sluggishly on the plaza outside the colonnade.

Two mule drivers were mending their pack saddles, pulling out the dried grass with which they were stuffed, carding it, and packing it in again to soften the saddles. The saddles now looked like the puffed-up mattresses of bridal beds sold by credit establishments. But when a saddle had been in use one day it would be just as hard and flat and broken-winded as the mattress of the bridal bed after the wedding night. The mules get used to this rapid decline in the softness and have to put up with it just as the young married couple have to—who do not complain of their miserable bargain to the furniture dealer in the hope that they may be allowed to get a week behind in their installments once in a while.

All along the colonnade there were unhappy-looking men leaning against the posts and pillars—Indians and mestizos who wondered why they were alive. They excited no more interest here than such men do anywhere throughout the vast Mexican Republic, and here as elsewhere the picture would not have been complete without these loungers and old-timers.

They spend the night somewhere—though no one can say where—and somewhere they pick up a tortilla—or even a tortilla stuffed with frijoles and chile—though nobody knows where or from whom.

If anyone asks them who they are and what they are doing there, they say that they are mozos, boys waiting to be engaged by travelers for the next stage. But if a traveler really wants a mozo, because his own servant has fallen sick, these fellows ask such a wage that the traveler could get three thoroughly experienced handymen at the price, if he had the time to look around. But skilled drivers and grooms do not hang about where engagements are only to be had by chance. Competent mozos, as soon as one job is at an end, go from fonda to fonda, finding travelers to whom they offer their services. These others, who hang about, wait, on the other hand, for a traveler in urgent need of a boy, so that they can name their price.

2

Don Ramón Velázquez, swinging in a hammock in the colonnade, was in need of a reliable and responsible boy for his horses. He reclined with one leg dangling over each side of the hammock and his hands clasped behind his head. With eyes wide open he was staring fixedly at the roof, as though trying to count the broken tiles.

He had already been three days in the place, held up for lack of a boy. He had got this far without one and had hoped to engage an Indian boy with the help of the secretary, but in this, owing to the secretary's absence, he had not been successful. He could not come to terms with any of the colonnade loungers; and apart from the wage, none of them wanted to go more than a two-day journey away from a place where he could laze away his time so pleasantly. Don Ramón would have had to pay not only for the two days out, but also for the two days of the boy's journey home again.

He had been on the point of coming to terms with one of them for the four days, but then the boy wanted a horse to ride and don Ramón would have had to hire one in the town. Not content with that the boy wanted to bring another boy, whom don Ramón would have had to pay as well, besides hiring a horse for him; for the first boy said he could not return alone because there were Indians on the road who were ready enough to commit murder when they had the chance.

At this don Ramón finally broke off negotiations. He decided to wait for the secretary's return to see if he could fix him up with a reliable boy. Otherwise, he would wait for a pack-mule caravan that would be going his way.

3

Don Gabriel was strolling along the colonnade when he suddenly heard himself hailed. "Hombre, don Gabriel, hijo de mi alma—my dear boy, what are you doing in this Godforsaken dog kennel?"

It was don Ramón who, hearing footsteps, had turned his head and at once recognized don Gabriel. He slipped to the ground and went up to embrace him in the Mexican fashion.

"I never expected to see you here. It's the last place on earth you can hope to find a civilized face under the brim of a hat. Cigarette?"

"Gracias," said don Gabriel, producing matches.

If anyone is given a cigarette, he must in return supply the match, in case the Swedish match monopoly should suffer and force legislation on Latin America, by which anyone who lights one cigarette from another or, worse, takes a glowing stick from the campfire to light it with, shall be punished with not less than two years' imprisonment. Already they have succeeded by adroit propaganda in preventing more than two people lighting their cigarettes with one match; for the third will be dogged by bad luck for the rest of his life and can only break the spell by hatching a revolution in one of the Latin American republics, with the object of replacing a president who is hostile to monopolies by one who favors them.

Don Ramón and don Gabriel sat down on a straight-backed rickety seat which stood in front of a fonda on the colonnade.

4

The two caballeros were old acquaintances. They had known each other from boyhood and had often since then spent days in the same place and the same inn together when they were buying up animals or engaged in other business, besides coming across each other on countless occasions on the road and in distant ranches on their journeys through the state.

"Are you still dealing in animals?" asked don Gabriel.

"No, not for a long time now," don Ramón replied. "There's not much to be made at it. Prices are bad. For some time now I have been in a far better line, where there's more profit, less uncertainty, and fewer losses. I deal in other cattle. I am an agent for the monterías, sometimes for the coffee plantations too. I recruit peons for contract labor. For every man I bring to Hucutsín and hand over there at the fiesta of the Candelaria, the companies pay me thirty pesos. And if I take the men on to the montería—fifty pesos a head there at the mahogany camp. No expenses—only my keep while I make the rounds of the fincas and ranches and the independent Indian villages to buy the fellows up. The only losses I have is when one of them dies on the journey through the bush or takes off and can't be caught, but that does not happen often. A fine business, I tell you, don Gabriel. A third, in some of the monterías half, of the peons are dead within the year and have to be replaced; so business is never slack. It's a hundred times better than dealing in cattle and pigs or horses and mules."

He flicked off the ash of his cigarette and waited for don Gabriel to say something. But don Gabriel was lost in thought. He saw the dawn of a golden future and he meant to seize his opportunity and find out in detail how to embark on this line of business. He hesitated to ask outright only because he was afraid it might not suit don Ramón to have a competitor and that don Ramón might put him on a false track if he asked too pointedly. He was wondering how he could lead him on to giving away the secrets of his method of doing business.

So he remained silent, until don Ramón at last slapped him on the knee. "And what are you doing nowadays, hombre? Still dealing in cattle, or is it goods now?"

"I have a post," don Gabriel replied, "secretario at Bujvilum."

"That's bad, amigo," said don Ramón, with a sour grimace. "There's not a bent peso to be made in these Indian villages.

They haven't got it. As soon as they can lay their hands on fifty centavos, they spend it on brandy. So how is a secretario to get on? I was had like that myself once—two years of it. Nothing but hard work and never knowing when a machete will get you in the guts or half a pound of scrap iron blow your head off your shoulders; and if you don't have to live in fear of your life, then you're only being too kind to the vermin and starving on the few miserable pesos you can squeeze out of your rotten country store."

"You're right, don Ramón," replied don Gabriel. "That's exactly how it is. But I can find nothing better."

"What are you doing in Cahancu?"

"Passing through," said don Gabriel, "taking a fellow to Jovel to be tried. He got drunk and killed a man. I wanted to settle it there on the spot but he had no money. I can't let it pass; it's too serious. If I'm to keep any authority over them, I must do something about it. Otherwise I'd have a murder every week, till it got so bad that not a dealer passing through would be safe and I wouldn't dare leave the house myself even in daylight, as happened to the secretary at Bicocac, till at last he had to have the soldiers around for a few weeks. You're not much better off with soldiers in the place—only more thieving and everlasting trouble over women."

"How old is the fellow you're taking to Jovel?" asked don Ramón.

"About twenty-eight, I would say."

"Strong and healthy?"

"Like a four-year-old bull," said don Gabriel.

"What would you have put his price at, I mean the multa for the murder, if you had settled it on the spot?"

"I'd have let it go at fifty pesos and welcome," said don Gabriel, "but he didn't have five, and no prospect of his ever finding the balance. He hasn't enough pigs and sheep, and his maize brings in next to nothing."

"Listen to me, amigo," said don Ramón after a pause for reflection. "Have you forwarded particulars of the case and said you were bringing the man to Jovel to stand trial?"

"No, I haven't," replied don Gabriel. "Anyway, a letter would have been there no sooner than I. We have no regular mail and I can only send letters when there's someone passing through or when someone from the village, who has enough sense to take a letter, goes to market."

Don Ramón slapped his friend once more on the knee. "Seems to me we can make a deal together. Sell me the boy for the multa, and ten pesos more for your expenses. I'll send the man with a gang bound for the monterías. I'll lose nothing by it. The sixty pesos I pay you for him will be booked to his account in the same way as the commission I get on each man I supply is booked against him."

5

Don Gabriel said neither yes nor no, and don Ramón thought that perhaps he was feeling a pang of conscience over selling the man. He hastened to blot out such damaging scruples before they became a real danger and threatened to spoil the deal.

"What will happen to the man at Jovel? I ask you. He'll get five or ten years in a penal settlement and won't survive three months. He'll never stand it—day in and day out between stone walls and iron bars. When he can't see the sky above him and trees and grass around him, he'll wilt and sicken in a few weeks. And there's no escape for him. Since he has to serve a sentence, he can just as well put it in at a montería, where his labor will be of more use than in prison or wherever else they send him. On a montería he will have hard labor, true, but he's tough and used to it. He'll be in the open under the sky and with others of his own sort. Between you and me, don Gabriel, you'll be dealing mercifully with the man by handing him over to me."

Don Gabriel made a gesture of indifference. "I have no interest in the man and no cause to deal mercifully with him or otherwise. What does an Indian matter to me?"

Here he broke off involuntarily. He saw Gregorio squatting with his wife and children at the moment when he had come on them saying good-by. Gregorio had never personally done him any harm. He felt a twinge of pity. It was not the pity he might have felt for another man, but the pity he might have felt for a suffering horse, which looked at him with sad eyes and the glimmer of a hope that a man might be able to help him, since horses knew no God to pity them.

It was certainly not, at least at this moment, the money that influenced don Gabriel in favor of don Ramón's proposal. He thought it over and came to the conclusion that it would in fact be better for Gregorio if he sent him to a montería instead of to prison. It was a question whether he would ever return from prison or a penal settlement. He might get five years or eight or even ten. It all depended on the judge's mood: he might have had a quarrel with his wife or a breakfast that had not agreed with him, or trouble with one of the women he kept, or he might have drunk too much the night before; or again this Indian prisoner might please him or disgust him, or he might be in the mood to make an example of him; or he might see a pretty girl in court who aroused kindly or severe or brutal feelings in him according to the impression she made and his notion of how he could best attract her attention to himself. On all these influences and contingencies turned Gregorio's fate: whether he would be acquitted or condemned to two or five or fourteen or twenty years' imprisonment, or shot.

An accused Indian never so much as thought of a lawyer to defend him. He had no money. As a formality, the State, so as to rank as civilized in the eyes of the world, provided counsel to defend him, whose duty was fulfilled when he had got up and said, "I plead extenuating circumstances for the accused." This said, he collected his papers and left the court in order to attend a trial from which there was something to be made; for he had to live and provide for his family.

Don Gabriel did not take all these details of the trial of an ignorant Indian cultivator into account, for they were not of any interest to him; but he knew that Gregorio, once in court, would be in a world as far away from anything he knew of as the other side of an undiscovered planet. The montería, in comparison, would be as familiar to him as his own village.

It did not take long for don Gabriel to convince himself that though in the eyes of the law it was an injustice to send Gregorio to a montería, it was a fate which he would prefer if he had the choice.

He sent for Gregorio.

"You know, muchacho," don Gabriel said to him, "what they'll do with you at Jovel—shoot you, probably."

"Yes, I know that, patroncito."

"And if they don't," don Gabriel went on, "they'll put you in jail for twenty years. You'll never see the sun or the sky. And they'll flog you as well."

"I know, patrón," Gregorio repeated.

"Here is a caballero, Gregorio," and don Gabriel pointed to don Ramón, "who is willing to take you along to a montería. There you will always be in the open, always in the forest. You'll see the birds and the animals. And you'll work there with other boys, Indians like yourself, with whom you can speak. The work will be hard, but hard work hurts nobody. There you will work out your multa and the contract money. In three years you'll be a free man again and you can go home to your woman and your children."

"I should like that, patroncito," said Gregorio.

"In three years it will all be forgotten and you will live as before in peace and happiness."

"Yes, patrón."

"Then you agree to go to the montería with this caballero, don Ramón?" asked don Gabriel.

"Yes, patrón."

"Then I'll see to it that you don't go to prison and we'll make the contract here and now," said don Gabriel.

6

The agreement was drawn up. Gregorio was debited with sixty pesos against his daily wage of two reales, or twenty-five centavos. This was the sum which don Gabriel received for handing him over—the fifty pesos multa and ten pesos costs. The thirty pesos which the company paid the agent for each laborer were also entered. Finally there were the twenty-five pesos for the stamp, which went into the pocket of the presidente of the municipalidad at Hucutsín and in return for which the contract received his official recognition. The mayor of Hucutsín, which was the last town before entering the region of the monterías, was then bound to arrest any man who broke his contract and escaped, and to hand him over to the company overseer, and the runaway in that case had the costs of his capture and return booked against him.

Don Ramón took out his list and wrote down Gregorio's name, the place he came from, his surety, Don Gabriel, and the sum with which his account opened.

Gregorio put a few strokes beneath his name as signature. He had now contracted a debt of one hundred and fifteen pesos. At the rate of twenty-five centavos a day that meant four hundred and sixty days' labor. Every shirt he would have to buy at the company's store during the period of his contract, every packet of tobacco, every straw hat, every blanket would be entered in a fresh account until the old account was worked off. As soon as the original account was met by four hundred and sixty days' labor, he would have the new one to work off; and this, owing to the necessary purchases he would make during his four hundred and sixty days, would exceed the original one set out in his contract. No laborer could leave a montería so long as he owed ten centavos to the company.

In this way the Indian, Gregorio, through the great goodness of his more instructed and Catholic fellow citizens and fellow men, was saved from the prison which others of his fellow Christians had built and were keeping ready for him. The hope which his wife, his children, his mother, his friends, and his village had of seeing him again would be fulfilled, accurately reckoned, in two thousand six hundred and thirty-four years, on the assumption that he bought nothing, not even a grain of salt, at the company's tienda more than was absolutely necessary.

7

The immediate benefits which accrued to don Ramón and don Gabriel were that don Ramón now had a reliable boy to accompany him at the bare cost of his food and that don Gabriel had sixty pesos in his pocket.

These sixty pesos, a larger sum than don Gabriel had had in his pocket for two years, fired his ambition. In his best days as a cattle dealer he had never made so much on one deal as he had now by dealing mercifully with an Indian.

Don Ramón treated don Gabriel as an old friend and made no secret of the business he conducted. He told him all about it in detail and of all the ruses which had to be employed to make it profitable. You had only to avoid open man-stealing. The Mexican citizen, he explained, was free. Slavery was strictly forbidden and severely punished. No Mexican citizen, whether of Spanish, mestizo, or Indian descent, could be kept or sold as a slave.

But debt was not slavery. A man, any man, was as free to contract debt as not to contract it; and if a debt was forced upon him, under threat of death or by torture, then it was not accounted a debt in law. Nobody compelled the Indian to get into debt, to drink, to set off fireworks in honor of the saints, or to buy his wife necklaces of glass beads and glittering earrings. There was no reason to call Mexico uncivilized because the dictatorship recognized debt and supported the creditor in exacting payments. He who has contracted a debt must pay it —that was good old Roman justice, respected by every country which called itself civilized. If the debtor could not pay in money he had to pay with whatever else he had. If he had nothing but his labor he had to pay with his labor.

"And over and above all that, and however you look at it," don Ramón went on, putting forward the just and Christian argument for his trade, "the monterías and coffee plantations must have labor if the prosperity of the country is to be maintained and the Republic of Mexico to have an honored and respected place among the nations of the world. Only work, hard, indefatigable, and unremitting work, can put our beloved Republic on top. These are the very words our president, don Porfirio, used in his New Year's proclamation to the Mexican people."

"Yes, you're quite right," don Gabriel agreed. "He has said it a hundred times—and it's the plain truth."

"You're right, amigo mio," said don Ramón. "Cattle dealing is a great deal more cruel and merciless. I have seen that often enough. You have a fine horse, gentle as a lamb, used to good treatment and kind words, and then the buyer comes along, a rough, brutal fellow, well known for his cruelty to animals. He looks the horse over, and the animal instinctively feels the man's brutality from the first touch of his hand. It trembles and sweat breaks out on it. But it is not asked whether it wishes to go with the dealer or not. The owner needs the money and must sell the horse. I cannot ask horses and mules whether they want to belong to this man or that. The idea is absurd. But I do ask a peon whether he will go to a montería or not. Didn't we ask Gregorio a moment ago whether he would rather go to a montería or to prison? We asked him and what did he say?"

"That he preferred the montería," said don Gabriel.

"Good. And that is how it is in the trade. It's all aboveboard. There's no compulsion. But all the same it is made clear that debts must be paid. The business depends on convincing the people that their debts must be paid and that you give them the opportunity of paying them."

8

Don Gabriel quickly took to it. He saw there was a fortune to be made, without real effort and without the need of allowing a margin for losses. He did not consider don Ramón any brighter than himself; and no intelligence was required. There were thousands of indebted peons and independent Indians in the district he was best acquainted with. In his own village alone there were more than a dozen who were deeply enough in his debt to give him the right to proceed against them in any way and by any means not expressly forbidden by the law. It was not illegal to offer them the chance of contracting with a montería as a means of freeing themselves from debt. On the contrary, the government was glad to see debts paid off, and even more glad that the companies who paid it well for licenses and concessions should be kept supplied with labor, so that production could be maintained and exports increased. Exports were necessary to the finances of the country and kept up the value of the peso on the money markets of London and New York. It was therefore a highly patriotic activity to supply the coffee plantations and the monterías with labor and to keep the supply constant; it was just as important as dying gloriously and miserably for the honor of your country assured of the joys of paradise.

Neither don Gabriel nor don Ramón would have hesitated a moment to serve his country or to put a bullet, or half a dozen bullets, through anybody whose patriotism was in question—their country first and last. And it couldn't hurt an Indian if he, too, by his labor in the monterías made his contribution to the fame and reputation and financial stability of the country to which he owed his life, his nationality, and the roof over his head. What is a man, even a poor ignorant Indian, without a country to belong to, without the right to call himself a member of the noblest, bravest, and most glorious nation on earth? He is nothing. A worm. A flea. A louse. A trembling reed broken by the storm. He has no place in the universe—a speck of dust driven hither and thither by every puff of wind.

It was a praiseworthy deed to release the Indian from the fate of being a speck of dust and to offer him the chance of helping to give Mexico a stable position on the money markets of the world. And it was pleasing in the sight of the Church too; for even the Church suffered when business was bad.

What had a lousy Indian to look forward to in his village? And what did he do for the glory of his country? He paid no duties or taxes—apart from the heavy tax on every glass of brandy he drank, on every cigarette he smoked, on every length of cotton he bought at a price which took into account twice over the heavy taxes the shopkeeper himself paid.

It was his duty to do more for the State than pay indirect taxes on his personal indulgences. This duty he could best fulfill by expending his strength to the last gasp in the holy and glorious task of increasing production for export.

To deal in cattle was mere self-seeking. To recruit Indian labor in order to put production on a competitive level was, on the other hand, a patriotic activity. As long as there is an unshakable conviction such as this, it is impossible to commit injustice or practice cruelty, to break up family life, to rob a man of all that life means to him. If you find the right formula, any crime can be justified and even sanctified in your own eyes and before the world.

9

Don Ramón had found the right formula, or rather, he had discovered it in the speeches of that great statesman, don Porfirio, and adapted it to his own purposes.

There was not a crime he did not have to commit in the task of rounding up labor, if he meant to thrive and to please his masters. Falsification of the accounts of Indians was the least of the crimes he committed in order to make them sign on.

Often he was generous and distributed brandy lavishly in some place where the secretary had the only brandy shop. This profited the secretary and the profit put him in a good mood.

When enough brandy had been given away to make the Indians quarrelsome, Don Ramón found ways of fanning the flame so that the quarrels ended in a free-for-all. As soon as enough men were involved, and a few killed, arrests were made. Next morning the secretary came down on each of the prisoners with multas of fifty to eighty pesos. Don Ramón paid the fines to the secretary and the men were saddled with the debt. The secretary then witnessed the contracts and don Ramón had netted fifteen or twenty men at one cast. If a man refused to contract himself, the secretary charged him with manslaughter and he was given the choice of going with don Ramón to the monterías or going before a judge. He always chose the montería.

Don Ramón did not always succeed in getting the men involved in a fight. Either they were more good-humored than suited him, or else—and this was more often the case—their wives and mothers employed every device they could think of to entice the men home when they were drunk. Once in their huts it was a simple matter for the women to cajole or force them to lie down and sleep off their debauch. After they were asleep they did not as a rule get up again until they were sober.

Sometimes, however, when the men were half drunk, he could get them to accept a sum of money as an advance on contract wages. Once they had taken the advance and named their sureties, the agreement was binding and he had his men.

There were agents, don Ramón among them, who made use of traveling traders to entice the men to buy more than they had the money to pay for. The agents were only too pleased to advance them any sum they liked against contract wages.

Often, with the help of unscrupulous and avaricious secretaries or other officials, a whole troop of Indians, who were on their way through a place to some market or fiesta, were surrounded and put under arrest. They were then accused of having an infectious disease, or of not being vaccinated, or of coming from a place under quarantine for cattle disease or smallpox. The Indians did not understand what it was all about, but when the tumult finally died down they found themselves peons in a montería from which there was no escape.

It might happen that a trader or a Mexican ranchero was murdered and robbed on the road somewhere—or else there was a rumor that it had happened, although nobody could say with certainty who the murdered man was, what he was called, where he had lived, and who had missed him. But articles which presumably had belonged to the victim appeared on roads traversed by Indians from independent villages, and the Indians picked them up, believing that they did not belong to anybody. On arriving in the next town they were arrested and searched. The articles were found on them, and the whole troop, often including the women and children, were charged with the murder and robbery and as a punishment handed over to an agent who carried them off to the monterías.

Or it might happen that someone had cut a telephone wire and stolen a few yards of it. The village of independent Indians nearest the place where the telephone wire had been damaged was surrounded by soldiers. All the men were arrested, three or four were hanged from a tree in the plaza, and two dozen strong and healthy young men were sent to the monterías.

There was no inquiry to find out who had cut the wire, though an agent or one of his underlings might well have been suspected of having done it. The Indians were charged and that settled it.

A high enough commission was paid to make it worthwhile to employ any device to recruit labor for the companies.

It did happen, certainly, that the agents went so far that even Mexican finqueros complained to the government of their brutality. Sometimes they were moved by humanity, but actually the finqueros and other owners of large properties were not interested in the fate of independent Indians. These independent settlements were against their own interests, for it sometimes happened that a few families of peons, who were tied to a finca and stocked it with laborers and so had a money value like any other cattle, left the finca as soon as they were free of debt and joined an independent Indian community. In this way the finqueros lost their laborers.

It was therefore an advantage for finqueros if the independent Indians were not too happy in their independence. The peons on a finca could not be recruited except with the permission of the finquero, and so they were safer from the agents.

Nevertheless, the large landowners had a certain inducement to complain sometimes of the agents' illegal and violent methods; for if the independent Indians were treated with too brutal a defiance of the law by merciless agents and avaricious officials, they abandoned their villages and, taking to the bush and jungle, formed marauding bands which made the roads unsafe and did not even respect the cattle and buildings of the finqueros. The damage which was caused before the government could send soldiers was so great that the finqueros had good reason to protest when the recruiting agents went too far. If complaints were too numerous and if their methods were found to be downright criminal, and if, in addition, paragraphs appeared in American newspapers giving particulars of the bar-

barous conditions in Mexico, then a few agents were arrested
and tried.

The agents had only one line of defense—patriotism: nothing
they did was done for business reasons, still less from greed,
but simply from genuine and unalloyed patriotism.

It was easy to prove it. Don Porfirio, the president of the
Mexican Republic, had, in exchange for hard cash, given
foreign companies licenses to denude the forests of valuable
timber which were one of the great resources of the country.
The more the national resources were developed the higher
was the country's credit on the international money market. It
was therefore a highly patriotic act to make these riches available to the rest of the world. But the companies could not exploit these riches if they had no labor; without labor the best
of concessions is worthless and the wealth of the country lay
idle in distant jungles and primeval forests. It was a matter of
patriotism to produce the laborers. If they did not come of their
own accord they had to be brought by force in order to promote the wealth of the country. It was their duty as citizens,
just as it was the duty of citizens to march through a barrage
if their country called upon them. The individual has no personal right in his own existence, still less to his labor, if the
State chooses to dispose of it otherwise.

No judge could withstand such arguments. The judge was
an official of the State, and his existence as a judge, his high
social position, and his prospects depended on the prosperity of
the country.

The trial ended in the judge's thanking the accused agents
in the name of the country for the hard and thankless work
they were compelled to undertake in the cause of its welfare
and prosperity. No Indian who had been a victim of forcible
methods was allowed to give evidence, because an Indian made
an unreliable witness and had no right to appear before a judge
except in the capacity of an accused person. He had nothing

but his labor that he could offer to the State. So it was his duty as decreed by God to increase the greatness and glory of his country by working in the monterías. Of course, the agents were told not to carry their recruiting methods too far, and to respect the personal rights of every Indian, who after all was a man and a baptized Catholic like everyone else.

The agents promised to do so, affirming at the same time that they had done nothing wrong or in defiance of the law, as anyone could convince himself from the books and the way the accounts were kept.

"You see," said don Ramón as he brought his exposition to a close, "the wheels are well oiled. I have pretty much a free hand. I am on excellent terms with the governor and with all other officials who could make themselves a nuisance. The jefe políticos, the local presidentes, and the chiefs of police have got to live too, and I never forget it. What does a lousy Indian matter? The world is no better or worse whether he lives or dies. But it is of some importance if he works. We only trouble about oxen and horses when they work; if they are no more use either to work or to sell, then their lives don't matter a cent."

10

It had been in don Gabriel's mind to go into this business on his own and to stand on his own feet from the start, but don Ramón's lengthy exposition decided him that it would be better to enter into a partnership. There might be snares and pitfalls with which you had to be familiar if you wanted business to go smoothly. He was clever enough not to let slip an opportunity which chance had so unexpectedly put into his hands.

"I have been thinking, don Ramón," he said, "while you have been explaining the business to me, and it seems to me that you would do well to take a partner. To come straight to the point: How would you like it if we two carried on the business together in the future?"

Don Ramón was taken aback by this sudden proposal, but as a man of business he saw at once that it offered many advantages. Don Gabriel was acquainted with districts which he scarcely knew at all. He was on good terms with many other secretaries of Indian villages and was a friend of the jefe político, and he knew all the finqueros of the districts where the market for buying Indian labor ought to be good. With don Gabriel as a partner don Ramón could greatly extend the sphere of his operations.

There was another reason why don Ramón felt tempted to take a partner. It was this: Don Ramón took his contract laborers only as far as Hucutsín, where he handed them over to the overseer of the montería on the day of the festival of the Candelaria after the contracts had been stamped by the mayor. His responsibility ended when he had got his men to Hucutsín by that day, and for every laborer delivered in good order he got thirty pesos. But if he took his gang as far as the montería which had commissioned him, he would get fifty pesos a man. Some of the companies paid as much as sixty pesos.

This journey with them through the jungle was, however, dangerous and fatiguing. He had only once undertaken it, and then he had employed Ladinos to help him, and these Mexican labor drivers were expensive. They were unreliable, too, when the Indians became refractory on the march. They had their fixed pay and would not bother very much if some of the men tried to escape. Having no interest in the booty, they saw no reason to put themselves out. With a partner it would be another matter. He would have a stake in the business and so would be on the watch day and night to see that not a man was missing.

Each man represented a lot of money. The agent had paid part of his debts, had agreed to pay the balance, and had perhaps paid an advance to the peon as well—to take the sting out of the contract. In addition, there was the cost of registering the contract at Hucutsín. Altogether, as much as a hundred and fifty pesos had been paid out, in some cases, on a single man. The capture of a runaway might last weeks, and even then he might never be found. He might perish in the jungle, or perhaps reach a village or a neighborhood where he would be able to hide among friends of his tribe who would keep him out of the way if any suspicious-looking Mexican turned up.

As for the business itself, two could run it more successfully than one. Each could go his own way in search of recruits, choosing the district he knew best. In that way more men would be got hold of in a shorter time. And it would also be easier to arrange to recruit labor for the coffee plantations. The plantations needed large numbers of laborers only at certain seasons, particularly during the harvest. These men were engaged for two or three months only; after the harvest or the weeding of the plantations they went back to their villages. They were more easily got hold of. It was often no trouble at all to find a thousand Indians for the plantations; after having worked on one the harvest before, they came forward of their own accord as soon as an agent they knew appeared in the village, as long as he had the sense not to spare the brandy and to be very insistent with his offers of wages in advance.

11

Don Ramón lost little time in thinking it over; but though he quickly decided to take don Gabriel into partnership, he did not forget to weigh the disadvantages.

One drawback was that don Gabriel might make himself a dangerous competitor in the districts don Ramón regarded as his own and then one fine day set up for himself. To compensate himself in advance for the losses don Gabriel's competition might cause him later, he made certain conditions before accepting the proposal.

"It's not a bad idea, don Gabriel," he said. "We're good

friends and we could work well together. But remember, you have to learn the business and I have to show you how it is done. It has taken a lot of trouble to get it going. I have many a shotgun and machete wound on my carcass as a perpetual reminder of my apprenticeship. I can teach you many a fine trick which will save you getting the same. It has never entered my head to take a partner. I can get along very well on my own. To prove it, I have carried on the racket a good number of years now and I've got a nice little pile to show."

"I believe you, don Ramón," said don Gabriel. He said it in a tone which carried conviction and scarcely concealed his fear that don Ramón might not be favorably disposed to partnership.

Don Ramón had gained a considerable knowledge of men in the course of his business. He had learned how to discover the weak side of finqueros who were unwilling to give up any of their peons and how to take them by surprise on an unprotected flank. He merely spent two or three days on the finca before getting down to business and made a thorough study of the finquero and of the terms on which he lived with his peons.

Being wide-awake and quick to notice anything that concerned his business, he detected instantly the vague fear behind don Gabriel's tone and immediately turned it to his own advantage without scruple. He raised the terms he had thought of proposing by two and a half pesos.

"Of course," he said, "if you really want to come in with me, naturally I can't say no to a good friend such as you are, don Gabriel. Muy bien—very well, we'll join forces. That's settled. But you will agree that if we go shares in the business I can't do it for nothing."

"Of course not. Of course not," don Gabriel broke in eagerly. "I see that. I am not such a fool as that. But between you and me, amigo mío, money is not very plentiful with me. At most I could put up a hundred fifty, or, if worse came to worse, two hundred. But that's the limit."

This admission was not lost on don Ramón. He had never thought of asking don Gabriel for a flat sum, but he accepted the offer. Never leave anything lying if it's there to be picked up and has the look of money.

"Well then, what I propose is this: You pay me a hundred and fifty as premium for joining the business. Further, for every man you bring along, you give me seven and a half pesos. That will leave you twenty-two pesos fifty a head; or, if we deliver the men ourselves to the montería, you will have from forty-two pesos fifty up to fifty-two pesos fifty. That will hold good for the first year of the partnership. For the second year you will give me five pesos a man. And at the end of two years we'll work together on equal terms; that is, you will take the full commission on every man you enlist on your own, and if we have to work the same district, as may happen, then we'll go halves, never mind how many men one or the other of us may have nabbed. Is that agreed, don Gabriel?"

"Agreed," said don Gabriel, "my word on it."

"And mine too, palabra de honor—word of honor as one caballero to another," replied don Ramón. "Then that's a bargain. When can you start, amigo?"

"The beginning of next month," said don Gabriel. "I haven't much to do at Jovel. Then I'll go to the district capital and hand in my resignation to the jefe político. I'll look around for someone to recommend to the jefe while I'm in Jovel, or my brother could take over until the jefe has found someone."

12

"Done. Then it's all settled," said don Ramón. "You can give me the hundred and fifty in two installments—fifty down to confirm the agreement and the rest at the beginning of next month. We'll meet here at Cahancu and plan our campaign. I'll induct you into the mysteries. You will make your headquarters at Chiilum and work the fincas and independent villages in all directions from there. I'll establish myself at Oshchuc. As soon as we have a hundred or a hundred and twenty men between us, we'll get under way—perhaps eighty would be safer. Too many's dangerous. I'll give you the proper dope for working it. Don't worry about that. Just don't let any sentimentality leak through into business. That's the main thing. It's a trade like any other. You were a cattle dealer long enough to know what that means. If you listened to every knock-kneed calf crying after the cow there would be no veal on the market. It's the market you have to think of, amigo mío. If you stopped to dry your eyes for every bleating calf, what would people have to put in their stews? People must have veal, and they must hang their rags in mahogany wardrobes. If the monterías get no labor, then the women must do without their beautiful polished mahogany gramophone cabinets and dressing tables. If we don't do the job for the monterías, others will. The world must be served and it is ready to pay for service. The world is not our responsibility. Keep that in your head and you'll have twenty men in a week. They sleep with their women all the year through and have a child a year. What's to be done with them all? It's better if we take them and make a few pesos on them than let the plague take them or leave them to kill each other. There's no more to be said. You have the government behind you. It must have taxes and the officials must have their pickings. What you make doesn't come out of their pockets. What's the good of these Indians? They're only a nuisance. They are born to work. Well then, do them the favor to tell them what they're here for. Pesos don't fall from heaven. You'll soon see how hard we have to work for them."

Don Gabriel listened attentively and let nothing escape him. Half of it he had learned already as secretary, so the rest was not difficult. Knowing this, he realized what a great and glorious future opened before him. He gladly paid don Ramón the fifty pesos down as his first contribution to the firm.

He bought two colored candles at one of the shops on the opposite side of the plaza, took them with him into the church and stood them up on the little table in front of the picture of the Holy Virgin. After lighting them and seeing that they burned properly, he knelt down, crossed himself, and devoutly reeled off a few *Ora pro nobis*. Then he crossed himself again, inclined himself three times before the picture, and left the church.

Gregorio meanwhile had washed down his new master's horse and given him a good heap of dried maize leaves.

8

  Don Gabriel left his wife behind at Jovel, where she took a house in preparation for their new life. She was overjoyed that her husband had given up his post as secretary and that she was not forced to return to that Indian village, where she had felt that an early death from sheer loneliness awaited her. In the town she was among her own kind. She praised her husband for being so quick to improve his position as soon as the opportunity of entering into an honorable and Christian business presented itself. She saw that their future was assured. On the strength of it she made large purchases of furniture, clothes, and household goods. She got unlimited credit when the shopkeepers heard what a secure and profitable line don Gabriel had gotten into.

Don Gabriel took an introduction from don Ramón to the representatives of the monterías in Tabasco, where they had their head offices, and got all the money he wanted; for just as the agents advanced money to able-bodied Indians, so the companies and their representatives were glad to advance it to the agents. An advance was better security than a written contract, for it had to be worked off, whether by Indians or agents.

141

The deeper an agent was in debt to the company, the more energetic he was in meeting its requirements.

2

Don Gabriel had been away two weeks and during this time his brother don Mateo had made the most of his time as secretary. He meant to show how authority should be exercised. In his opinion, his brother had no idea of it.

He had six men in jail, having sold them all the brandy they wanted when they were already drunk. He had fined them each five pesos for disturbance of the peace and was now waiting until either they or their relations paid the money so that they could be set free.

He had not let them sit it out in the clink doing nothing. He had sent them into the bush to cut wood which he intended to sell when the opportunity presented itself.

He had had fifteen prisoners in all during the two weeks, but the others had paid their fines. That was forty-five pesos in his pocket. He understood the art of government.

Something else had occurred in don Gabriel's absence, for when he returned he found his brother with his arm in a sling.

"Where did you get that?" asked don Gabriel.

"Where do you think I'd get it, hermanito?" said don Mateo. "One of your lambs tried to kill me with a machete, but I was just in time to catch it on my arm. You see what a gang of murderers you've turned them into. If I'd been secretary here as long as you have I'd have brought them to heel by this time. Then this would never have happened, I can tell you that."

"What did the fellow want to kill you for?" asked don Gabriel.

"Nothing. Nothing whatever. They're a lousy pack of murderous rebels. That's what it is."

Don Gabriel was quite aware that the people there killed no

one for no reason, but he asked no more. He knew his brother
well enough to realize he would not get a straight answer.

3

When the chief heard that don Gabriel was back he came to
greet him, and when they were alone don Gabriel heard the
story.

A young Indian girl whose father and mother were dead and
who lived with an uncle and aunt came to the cabildo to buy
matches. She pleased don Mateo and he told the Indian jefe
that the girl was to come to the cabildo every day to cook for
him, as he could not stomach the food cooked by the woman
who worked for don Gabriel and his wife.

The girl had been in the house only two days when don
Mateo assaulted her after having tried for hours to cajole her
with ribbons from the shop. His violence was not much more
successful. The girl ran screaming from the house with her dress
torn.

Indian girls are so modest that they would never speak to
anyone of such an occurrence, unless it were to their mothers.
But everyone in the place, particularly her closer connections
in the family group, knew at once what must have happened.

The girl had a boy friend to whom she had been promised
for two years. The boy was working hard to make money
for the wedding present to the girl's uncle. On the day of the
assault he was in the bush, catching snakes—their dried skins
fetched good prices.

That night when don Mateo stepped outside the door, a man
leaped at him out of the darkness with his machete. As the door
was open, don Mateo just had time to slip under cover and that
saved his life. But he got a deep gash in his arm.

The girl's boy friend as well as her uncle were with the
casique in his hut at the precise time that don Mateo was
wounded. That was very wise of them. They had paid a

friendly visit to the casique because they were the two who would be suspected of the attack. Meanwhile the matter was taken in hand by another member of the family group on whom no certain suspicion could fall; for though those who are related by family ties are very well known to each other, it is difficult, if not impossible, for those who do not belong to the village to make out who belongs to which family group and which boys and men are related by blood.

4

"I never thought," said don Gabriel to his brother, "that you could be such a bungler. You surely know enough about these people and their ways by now not to have made such a stupid mistake as that. It's never safe to meddle with their girls. An Indian respects them, because he knows that his life depends on it. You can count yourself lucky to have come out of it as well as you have. Even so, it's high time you cleared out. Your life is no longer safe in this place or near it—once outside the walls of the cabildo."

Don Mateo seated himself on the table, his legs dangling, and made a wry face. "So it's come to that, has it? You want to chuck me out. A nice brother you are. Never mind, I was going to leave anyway. Don Belisario, the Syrian trader, passed through the day before yesterday. He had good news for me. The chief of police, whom I had the shooting match with at Balún-Canán, has got himself transferred to Huixtla, because his compadre there is mayor. Don Belisario told me too that the chief bears me no grudge. He's been on his feet again for a long time now. I'm leaving the day after tomorrow for Balún-Canán. There'll be a job for me there, I've no doubt. Perhaps I'll take on the chief of police spot myself now. I'll soon have an iron in the fire. Don't you worry."

"There was no question of chucking you out," don Gabriel said quietly. "You know well enough I would not let you down.

I only meant it was better for your own sake if you went. I've heard enough today. You've made the place too hot for yourself. There's not a man here who isn't on your track. I don't know how you've managed it in two weeks and I don't want to know. You can have the money you've made in my absence for your journey."

Don Mateo laughed loudly. "You didn't think I was going to give it to you, did you? You must be weak in the head to think that. I earned it, I can tell you. If you followed the example I've set you these two weeks you could buy the best finca in the whole state in two years. But you were a born fool and a fool you will remain. You're past redemption. I don't mean it nastily. I'm only telling you and you may as well know it."

Don Gabriel had said not a word to his brother about his having become a recruiting agent for labor—a job that don Mateo would have jumped at. He had thought of telling him, but now that their talk had taken this turn he found it wiser to say nothing. Besides, it might have put ideas into don Mateo's head and perhaps brought an awkward rival into the field.

5

Don Mateo was unable to start out the morning he had meant to for lack of a boy to accompany him. Everyone whom don Gabriel tried to get hold of found some good excuse: either he had to work on his milpa—his maize patch—or he had a lame foot, or his wife was sick—there was something to detain each of them. Don Gabriel saw from this that not one of the men meant to accompany his brother. He offered half a peso a day for the journey there and back, but even that did not tempt them to go with don Mateo.

That afternoon another Syrian merchant came through on his way to Achlumal. From there to Balún-Canán it was only two days on horseback, and there were many ranches, farms, and even a few small villages on the way. The country was sparsely inhabited only as far as Achlumal. So don Mateo decided to travel with this trader, don Elias, as far as Achlumal and from there to continue alone, unless he got a boy in Achlumal.

Don Gabriel did not hear until four years later, when he chanced to meet don Elias at Yalanchén, what occurred on the way to Achlumal. Don Gabriel had lived all those years in the belief that his brother had arrived safely at Balún-Canán. He had never expected don Mateo to write or telephone him of his safe arrival. Besides, he left the place himself shortly after don Mateo's departure, so that a letter from his brother, if he had written, might easily have missed him.

6

Don Mateo set out with don Elias and the trader's two pack mules at the break of day. The road as far as Hucutsín was very lonely, but they got there without incident, arriving early in the afternoon on the third day. Don Elias had business to attend to there and some money owed him from previous sales to collect, so they spent the night in Hucutsín.

Next day they started out again for Achlumal. It was a lonely road. There were a few large fincas, so large that it was a four-hour ride from one finquero's house to the next. A few small ranches belonging to Indians or mestizos lay off the road. The travelers had crossed the Jatate River and were riding along a narrow path through the bush when they heard the crackling of twigs, sometimes to their left, sometimes to their right.

At first they thought stray cattle were in the bush in search of the leaves of trees and shrubs which they preferred to the wiry grass of the pastures. But they soon realized that the sounds came neither from cows nor deer and reached the conclusion that they were being followed.

Don Elias was alarmed. He suspected that thieves from Hucutsín were on his track to rob him of the money he had collected. He wanted to turn back, but don Mateo said there was no point in that, for if they were after his money they could attack him just as easily if he went back as if he went forward. There was nothing to do but ride on.

They rode together for the sake of company, and the two pack mules, who had often been that way and knew the trail well, went peacefully on ahead of them. Don Mateo continued talking without apparent concern, but he kept a sharp lookout on the bush on either side, hoping to catch a glimpse of the men who were dogging them.

He was sorry now that he had chosen this trader for his companion. He was convinced that the bandits were only after the trader's money, but that as soon as they came to a suitable spot they would murder him too as a witness. There was no doubt in his mind that he would have done far better to have traveled alone. The pack mules, owing to their loads, went only at a walk, and so he could not trot quickly through the danger spots, where the path ran between banks, and be ready to break into a gallop if anyone barred his way.

"There!" he cried out suddenly, breaking off his talk. "I saw one of them. It was an Indian with a shotgun."

Don Elias tried to take heart. "Then that's all right," he said cheerfully. "It's only some Indians from a finca, out hunting. They're on the track of a deer, probably."

Don Mateo pulled out his revolver and, taking his reins in his left hand, held it in his right ready to shoot. When they had ridden on for another hundred paces, he looked quickly to the right.

"Stand still, you cabrón, you son of a whore!" don Mateo shouted. "Come out of there or I'll shoot!"

The movement in the tangle of leaves and branches died instantly. Don Mateo fired three shots in quick succession into the dense foliage that had just been stirring.

"I believe I know the man," he said half to himself. "He's one of the Bujvilum fellows. I recognized him by his hat—I couldn't catch sight of his face, damn him. Perhaps I got him though."

He got off his horse and went to the spot he had fired at. He parted the branches, but there was nothing to be seen except that somebody had in fact been standing there, for there were twigs so freshly broken they were still moving.

Before mounting again he tightened his horse's girth, and then, pushing out the three empty cartridges, put in three new ones. While he was still busy with his revolver he saw a movement in the bush, at the left of the path this time, and called out to don Elias, who was already riding on.

"I'm right, don Elias. They're from Bujvilum. I know them both."

He fired four shots into the bush and then plunged in to see if he had hit the man. This time he did not appear again at once, but called back, "I'm after them."

Don Elias rode on. He was sure don Mateo was seeing things, mistaking Indians from around there for Bujvilum Indians and shooting wildly for no reason. Besides, he had to follow his pack mules in case they left the path and broke away. They might shed their packs and lose themselves. He was sure that don Mateo would soon follow, for the fellow knew the way and was used to traveling through bush.

All the same when he came to a finca at midday he stopped and waited. He waited until nightfall and then unloaded his mules and stayed the night, still hoping that don Mateo would appear.

"Don't you worry about don Mateo, don Elias," said the finquero. "He won't come to any harm. I can tell you what has happened. His horse was scared by the shooting and ran away. Don Mateo has gone after it, naturally. He won't want to lose his horse, nor his saddle and bridle. That's as clear as daylight. He'll stay the night in some little rancho back there. He's not a child."

"But then, there were those muchachos," don Elias objected.

"Ghosts," said the finquero, filling up their glasses with comiteco. "The muchachos harm nobody. All good boys. I've lived here fifty years. Never any trouble. I ride alone through the bush far and wide. Lord knows how far."

"But don Mateo shouted out that he knew the fellows and that they were from Bujvilum," said don Elias.

The finquero laughed louder than ever. "You can see for yourself that that's not right, don Elias. You can't tell me that those Indians would make a trip of three or four days from their pueblo to follow don Mateo. If they were really after him they'd have ambushed him on the road an hour away from their village. They're not the fellows to travel farther than they need."

Don Elias, however, was not satisfied. He spent the whole of the next day at the finca. The finquero sent three peons back along the road to see if they could come upon don Mateo's tracks.

The boys came back in the evening. They said they could see from the horse's hoofprints where don Mateo had dismounted, for close by the numerous hoofprints of a standing horse they had seen the prints of don Mateo's boots as well. They had searched the bush at that spot, but had discovered nothing more than that some Indians wearing sandals had left their tracks there. Finally they had made sure that the tracks of the horse led back in the direction of Hucutsín.

"Then there is nothing to worry about," said the finquero. "It was only some Indians hunting in the bush. And the horse, as I said, was frightened by the shots and ran away, with don Mateo after it. He may find that it has gone all the way back to Bujvilum, where it was out at grass during these last weeks.

There's only one thing for him to do if he wants his horse and saddle again, and that is to hire a horse in Hucutsín and ride back to Bujvilum. It's a question whether he will take this road again. There are two other ways to Balún-Canán from Bujvilum besides this one. So if you mean to wait for him you may wait a long time. Let's have another comiteco, don Elias."

As the mystery now seemed to don Elias to be cleared up, he worried no more about don Mateo's disappearance. It happens so often that a horse runs away and returns to its own pasture days later, or even joins a sympathetic drove of horses on a strange pasture, while its rider is compelled to retrace his steps without being able to warn his companions, who have ridden on believing that he is following them, that don Elias cannot be blamed for having found the finquero's explanation perfectly satisfactory. When he finally reached Achlumal there were so many business cares awaiting him that he soon forgot whatever doubts remained in his mind about don Mateo's fate. When he met don Gabriel four years later and heard that he did not know where his brother was all his doubts returned.

7

Don Mateo was never seen again, nor did anyone ever hear anything further of him and his fate. His horse was never found on any pasture at Bujvilum. If it had been found anywhere in the neighborhood with its saddle on its back, the finder would no doubt have made his find known.

Of course, the horse might have lost its saddle—the girth might have frayed or broken. It is possible too that the horse came to a small and isolated rancho and that the ranchero caught it and waited a few weeks for its owner. After that he would have put it out to pasture and taken charge of the saddle and bridle. As time went by without his hearing anything of a possible owner he would finally have forgotten that they were not his own. Since he was far from any town he would have had a good enough excuse for saying nothing about his find, for he was not obligated to undertake a long journey to report it. It would not have been very difficult to alter the brand. A pious Christian should not look askance at any welcome gift God sends him. It would be a sin to do so.

When don Gabriel heard what had transpired on his brother's journey with the Syrian trader, he knew without a doubt what don Mateo's fate had been. After four years he did not mourn him long. It had happened too long ago to shed tears over now. He did not even bother to search the bush at the place where don Mateo had last been seen, in the hope of giving him a Christian burial. He knew it would be wasted labor to look for the body so long afterward. It was certain to have been burned to prevent dogs out hunting with their master from coming on the scent and to keep vultures from betraying the spot where it lay; and by this time the scrub would have grown so thick over the place that little hope remained of finding the body.

To have made the journey to Bujvilum and questioned the people in the hope of finding out which men had been absent from the village on that day would have been even more fruitless than searching for the body; for if the men had followed don Mateo for such a distance in order to avoid murdering him near their own neighborhood, it was clear enough that their plan of revenge had been well thought out. Even if a ranchero had chanced to see them on the road near the place where it was executed, they would not have needed to fear discovery. No one would have known them so far from their own village. And what good would it have done to have discovered the culprits after so long an interval? It would not have brought don Mateo to life again whether they were shot or not.

So don Gabriel consoled himself for the loss of his brother, and as a tribute to his memory he paid eighteen pesos to have a Mass said for his soul in the cathedral at Jovel. With that don Gabriel had amply discharged his duty toward him.

8

On the morning that don Mateo rode away from Bujvilum, don Gabriel went to the jail and let out the men whom don Mateo had kept under arrest. He asked them what they were there for.

Each said the same. They had all been drunk, but not badly; they had neither struck nor wounded anyone with a machete.

When don Gabriel had satisfied himself that not one of them was in a position to pay even a peso as multa, owing to the poverty of their soil and the size of their families, he employed them in the cabildo in packing up the scanty belongings he and his wife had brought with them when he first took up his post there. He then told them that instead of paying a multa as punishment for their offenses they were to carry the things they had packed to Jovel. It would have cost don Gabriel a good sum if he had had to transport his effects to Jovel on hired mules—a journey of five or six days. In this way his prisoners were of more benefit to him than if each had paid a fine of five pesos. He had reason to congratulate himself on a stroke of good business.

Then he made up his account of taxes received. He did it so well that the government's share was only nominal; for there was a jefe político to think of, too. That gentleman's takings were largely made up of the comfortable percentages which the secretaries and other officials, who owed their positions to him, had to deduct from the taxes and various levies they raised. That is why, when you got into office yourself, you made officials of your friends and relations.

Because don Gabriel had to feed the jefe político, he cooked up the accounts for the government inspector of taxes so cleverly that the jefe político's share was very much larger than the government's He left it to the jefe político to put himself right with the revenue office. There would be no examination of the accounts, for that sort of thing only meant work and made enemies on every side.

Don Gabriel allotted a considerable sum to the jefe político on account of tours of inspection, which apparently had so frequently brought his chief to Bujvilum. In truth he had only once been to the place during don Gabriel's tenure of office, because he was afraid of the food and the rats on the small ranchos where he had to stay. He arranged such tours as he could not avoid so that he spent the night in the large and prosperous fincas, and when he came on a particularly comfortable one he often spent several days with the finquero and made it appear from his report that he had journeyed far and wide for four long days and only returned again to the finca on the fifth. The finquero and cattle dealers with whom he talked supplied him with material for his reports on the places he was supposed to have inspected.

When the jefe político received don Gabriel's accounts he found them so entirely to his satisfaction that don Gabriel would be able to go to considerable lengths in the recruiting of Indian labor before he need fear a lecture on the law and the constitution or any interference at all from that personage.

It would not have been to defend the constitutional rights of the Indians, who were citizens as he was, that the jefe político would have talked of the law and the constitution. It would have been merely with the intention of entangling the agent in the meshes of the law, so that he would have had to buy himself loose. Why shouldn't the jefe político and other officials make a bit too if these agents made so much in a few years that they bought themselves large fincas and lived on them in the style of *grands seigneurs?* It was a hard and thankless task to have to cement the foundations of the State and make of it an ordered and prosperous enterprise, secure against any shock.

9

Nobody could accuse don Gabriel of letting the grass grow under his feet. He was a capable and industrious man of whom Church and State might be proud. All that he had lacked had been the right opportunity and the foundations to build on. If you have no shop and no goods it is not much help to be a good salesman. There must be something there to start from.

As soon as his reports were done and his tax accounts put in such a shape that it would have been difficult for any inspector, however zealous he might have been, to detect the errors which favored the author of them, he set about enlivening the promising market, which opened before him not only with goods but with clients. It is the sign of a good merchant to grasp a situation and to exploit it the moment it presents itself. It can be studied later when the money has been banked. It is always better to look into the wrongs and injustices and brutalities which may have arisen in the course of the deal and even, possibly, to regret them, when the paint is dry. Then the blush of shame or the pang of regret at least cost no cash. Shame and regret can be soothed and put to sleep by lighting a dozen candles before the statue of the Virgin. And since all men are by nature weak, the señor Cura, good man, who cares for the soul, soon puts the matter right. He will not forget to say at the right moment how much it costs to launder the soul. There are no sins which cannot be forgiven if you take the trouble to go to the man who, by virtue of inward grace, is on intimate terms with the heavenly powers and knows to a nicety what God thinks and does in every contingency that can arise.

10

Don Gabriel summoned the village chief to the cabildo. He poured him a glass of brandy.

"Yes, I am leaving you, don Narciso," said don Gabriel.

"That is a great pity, don Gabriel," said the chief. "We could have worked well together."

"True, true," replied don Gabriel. "Not many secretarios are such good men as I am and not many mean so well to the poor Indio as I do. Have another, don Narciso."

"Gracias," said the chief.

"Well, there it is," don Gabriel went on. "But what's to be done about the money so many of the people of the place owe me? That's what I want to know."

The chief looked puzzled. "It is hard to say, don Gabriel."

"You will agree, don Narciso, that I cannot forgo so much money. A debt is a debt. I will say nothing of all the multas which are due to me; or rather, I will speak of them. I will show you, jefe, what a good heart I have and how sincerely I feel for the poor ignorant Indio. I'll let them off their multas."

"They will be very pleased to hear that," said the chief. "It is a very gracious act on your part, don Gabriel. It will make the whole village your friend forever."

Don Gabriel needed their friendship. It gave him the theme for the tune he now wished to play.

"But the other debts are hard cash from my pocket. I cannot let them off those."

"You certainly cannot do that, don Gabriel," the chief agreed.

"Well, you know all the fellows here who owe me money, don Narciso." Don Gabriel took out his notebook and read the names and the amounts against each.

When he had come to the end of the list he said, "Which of them can pay me what he owes? Not one. And none of their sureties can pay either. It would take some of them four or five harvests. Now I'll make a fair offer, don Narciso. Pick me out ten strong young fellows, friends or sons or nephews or relations of the debtors and their sureties. These ten young fellows will take the whole debt on themselves. The muchachos can reckon that out with their family groups. We'll choose fellows who want to marry and don't have the money for the marriage gift to the girl's father and to pay for the wedding. Now there's a friend of mine, a good and honorable man. Talk about a good heart—that caballero has a heart for the poor Indian like a shining star in heaven, and even far better. And this caballero wants some strong fellows who know how to work."

"But it wouldn't be for the monterías?" said the chief nervously.

"What an idea, don Narciso!" said don Gabriel, putting up his hand as though to ward off an insult. "No, no, the people are not for the monterías. My friend, this caballero whom I spoke of, needs the people for a finca. You see, don Narciso, the caballero has bought a finca from the state—cheap. But the finca is a new one. It is only jungle at present. That's why he was able to buy it so cheap. Now he has to clear the jungle before he can start with his finca. The finquero wants to plant it with coffee or cocoa and, of course, maize."

"Oh, a cafetal," said don Narciso with a sigh of relief.

"Exactly. That's exactly what it is, a coffee plantation. You have guessed rightly, don Narciso."

"If the boys are to go to a coffee plantation," said the chief, "that is a different thing. That makes it much easier to get hold of the boys. I can put in a good word for that with the men."

"That is just why I wanted to discuss it with you, don Narciso," said don Gabriel. "As jefe, you can put things before the family groups. The boys will go if you give the word. They will agree that it's the best and only way out for the village if I am to get my money. These fellows will take over the debt, and, of course, the costs of the contract too, you understand. They will work off the debt on this new finca and they can easily make something for themselves besides. Then when they come back and want to marry they will have enough money over to buy themselves sheep and goats. They will get forty centavos a day—if they work well, even fifty. Think of that—half a peso a day. That makes in a year a hundred and eighty good round pesos."

"A heap of money for young fellows who want to marry, that I must say," replied the chief.

"It is a mountain of money, I tell you, don Narciso. Drink another copita, and tell the people about it. You know the names of those who are in my debt and how much they owe, and you can arrange with the men at your leisure how much of the whole debt each of the young fellows will undertake. In a year, or let us say in a year and a half, they can all be back again, and then there can be two weddings a week here and no one in debt and every man in the village will be able to sell his maize and his pigs and his wool to anyone he likes and for whatever price he can get. And I will say this too: the people may sell their pigs and their wool, and whatever else they have, free of all tax as soon as the boys have actually taken the debt upon themselves and have all arrived at this new finca."

"Good," said the chief. "I will now go and consult with the men and tell them what you have proposed."

"Right, don Narciso," replied don Gabriel.

When the chief had reached the door, don Gabriel said, "One moment, don Narciso. We have always been good friends. I still have a good deal of aguardiente. There may be thirty liters or so on my hands. I am leaving in a few days and I don't think I will sell much of it by that time—at most three or four liters. I will give what is left as a token of friendship. You can sell it here yourself. I don't suppose a new secretary will come so very soon, and as long as there is no secretary here you can sell as much brandy as you like."

Narciso did not show whether he was pleased or not with this gift. Neither by word nor gesture did he express what he really thought. He merely said, "Gracias," and he said it with the same simple courtesy he would have used if offered a chair.

11

Like so many simple people who can neither read nor write and who know still less of higher mathematics or the graph of emotion in a dissected play of Shakespeare, the chief had all the same the important gift of being able to see through his opponent and to sense at once that his behavior was not as simple as it appeared to be.

Don Gabriel could not in the few days he was still to be there sell the brandy he had in his store. If he had been able to he would not have given it away. But he did not especially want to take it with him either, for he had enough things to transport already. And if he had to give it away what better use could he make of it than to bribe the chief?

The secretary was baiting a hook with which he meant to catch something. But however hard Narciso thought when the secretary made his offer, he could not figure out what the ruse was. To clear a piece of jungle and prepare the ground for coffee planting was a straightforward job with an end in sight. Besides, a new finca promised much, particularly if its owner was a good and friendly master, inclined perhaps to take on young Indian married couples as peons and to offer them a life which, even though laborious and deprived of liberty, offered all the same more security than the barren ground of their independent village. If the families in the village grew too large the land allotted to each family would of necessity become ever smaller, and as the land belonging to the community was in any case thirsty and barren ground—otherwise it would never have been left to an Indian community—the livelihood of the people in the village was bound to become more and more precarious as new families arose.

The treatment of peons on a new finca is always better than on a finca that has already been in existence for several centuries. The finquero wants to increase the number of the families which produce peons for him. He tempts them to leave their independent villages by allowing them to choose their own plots from the virgin land. So long as it does not interfere with his own enclosures, he also leaves them a free hand to choose whatever parts of the jungle they would like to cultivate for themselves. The virgin soil of the jungle is extremely fertile and gives a rich return to the families who work it.

In order to bind the new families to him the finquero gives them building material for their huts; he sells them young pigs and goats and sheep cheaply; he gladly offers them advances in cash and makes it easy for them to work these off. The news quickly spreads throughout the independent villages and the finquero soon has more families on his new finca than he had thought of accommodating. As soon as he has applications from more families than he can make use of and as soon as the earlier settlers have begun to form clans with the new ones and to intermarry, and as soon as they have all begun to feel attached to the earth they have won from the jungle and would hate to be parted from, then the finquero begins to exploit his peons just as the peons on the centuries-old fincas are exploited.

The same laws that produce the slow pauperization and enslavement of industrial workers in all civilized countries can be seen at work here too. When a new branch of industry is developed as the result of a new discovery and holds out the promise of large profits, high wages and enticing rates for piecework are offered to workers in order to draw them from every rank of labor, even from agriculture, with the object of developing this new branch of industry to the highest pitch in the shortest time. Once the development is complete this branch of industry has already absorbed all the labor it can, but workers still flock to it and press so heavily on the established work force that the favorable conditions are reversed. The workers who have fallen into the trap cannot return to their original occupations, either because they have altered in the course of time or other workers coming up from lower economic levels have taken their jobs.

It is just the same with the development of a new finca—the first five years give the peon a magnificent return in every way. It is the profit of these first five years that tempts many independent Indians to become peons on a new finca. They come in the belief that they can always leave when conditions and the treatment they receive worsen; but as soon as conditions begin to deteriorate they find they cannot go. Either they are by that time so deeply in debt that they are not free to go, or else they have become so attached to their new home that from reasons of kinship and other sentimental feelings the power of choice has left them.

12

It was, in fact, an excellent ruse which don Gabriel had employed as a prelude to his new business. The chief had no means of knowing that don Gabriel was playing a villainous trick on him. He trusted don Gabriel's word because it did not occur to him that an official, the secretary of the place, whom he had known for almost a year, could be so unscrupulous as to speak of the starting of a coffee plantation or a finca when he meant a montería. And yet there was something in don Gabriel's offer that made the chief mistrust him. But, however far mistrust may go, it comes at last to its limit: there comes a point when it gives way, because every man has a heart and a soul and a feeling for his fellow men. In the case of an Indian, whose life is close to nature, who bases all his acts and his dealings among his own folk on pure trust, who has no stamped documents because none can read them, the limit at which mistrust gives out is much sooner reached than in the case of civilized people, who, unless the receipt is produced, swear without the flicker of an eyelid that money they have received was never paid. So it was impossible for the chief to suppose, even for a moment, that don Gabriel, whom he saw sitting there before his eyes and whom he regarded as an honorable official, could have betrayed him in so miserable a fashion without the faintest sign of shame or confusion.

It is true that the chief was not entirely happy about the present of brandy he was offered. But he could not see the bribery, and unless he had felt that it was a bribe he could not have concluded that a trick was being played on him.

While he walked across to the village to consult with the men, he could not get his mind off this present of the brandy. Nor could he get away from the simple explanation, which seemed to him perfectly natural, that don Gabriel gave him the brandy because he thought it wiser to leave it behind in the hands of the chief than in those of any other man. Don Gabriel might have distributed the brandy among the men of the place, but they would have got drunk and this might have brought mischief on the village. Since don Gabriel had not done this but given it instead into his charge to deal with according to his discretion, the chief believed that don Gabriel was really the friend of the village and wished to prevent trouble that might have had ugly consequences.

Each man, don Gabriel and the chief, saw the gift in a different light owing to the difference in their racial characters, in their circumstances, and their environment. Don Gabriel meant it as a bribe to oil the business better, and he supposed the chief took it as a bribe. The chief supposed it was given to him as the man responsible for the people and out of friendship for the place—perhaps, too, as a parting gift of friendship. For these reasons Narciso had not simply refused the gift.

13

The chief summoned the men of the village and put forth the secretary's proposal in the light in which it appeared to him. He was as honest with the men as a good father is with his children. He told them that it was an excellent prospect for young married couples and, for the next five or eight years at least, offered a better life for them than the village could provide—for the best land at the disposal of the village was allotted to the older families who had many mouths to feed, while newly established families, according to tradition and custom, had to be content with what was left. This never gave rise to any dispute, for it was recognized by all as not only the just but the only and natural arrangement.

The men who were consulted agreed that there was nothing improper in the secretary's proposal. It was only natural and right that the secretary should recover the money he had lent. Therefore, it had to be produced somehow. Those who had stood security for a relation or a friend were also in agreement. They insisted that the debtors should discharge their obligations. No one had forced them to get into debt. The Indians did not consider it meanness on the part of the creditor that the originally small debts had grown to considerable sums owing to don Gabriel's peculiar methods of reckoning interest. They knew well enough that not even a peso was lent to any man, least of all to an Indian, at a low rate of interest, when the security was so uncertain that the creditor was always in danger of losing the principal. Interest at 500 per cent was quite just and moderate in the case of such unstable financial assets as an Indian possessed.

To make your views go down with any assembly you must be thoroughly at home with the circumstances in which you find yourself. High-sounding phrases about the universal and eternal and incontestable rights of man only make you ridiculous on such occasions, because even the most beautiful commonplaces are either quite out of order or can only be brought into accord with the matter under discussion and the cold reality of daily life by acrobatic contortions and manipulations.

Even a simple Indian can see that—even better sometimes—

than many a civilized worker, who believes that the whole world will be bathed in sparkling sunshine as soon as all men combine to believe in the one and only program.

The council of Indians came to the conclusion that the acceptance of don Gabriel's proposal was the only way of meeting a difficult situation. If the secretary was leaving the place he had to collect all outstanding debts. Nobody could ask him to cancel them. Nobody expected him to. He had the right to demand payment. Everyone, debtors included, recognized that. No objection could be raised to his asking for the money. He had not forced his money or his goods on anybody. When the debtors had been in need of the money or the goods they had been very glad to receive them on credit, so they had no right now to make difficulties when the money had to be paid back, all the less as the day on which the payment was due had in every case long passed.

The men agreed among themselves which of the boys should share the responsibility for the debts. There was no necessity to bring the influence of the family groups to bear upon them before they would enter into the contracts don Gabriel offered. Several boys on whom no part of the debt fell, because there was no older man in debt either in their own families or in the families of the girls they wanted to marry, came forward of their own free will as soon as they heard that the work was for a finca which was just being started. They saw the chance of earning money more quickly and so of having a home of their own sooner than if they stayed in the village.

At one blow don Gabriel got twenty strong and healthy young men from the village—twice as many as he had bargained for. He had made a good start in his business. He could scarcely wait to see the expression on don Ramón's face when he reported such a catch to him at their next meeting.

14

When, a few months later, the boys found they were being taken to a montería, they protested against the contracts.

They had put their signatures to what don Gabriel gave his word was in the contracts, but was not there at all. Not one of them could read; the only man they knew who could read was their secretario, don Gabriel. They might have asked a licenciado to read the contract to them, but they would have had to pay the lawyer; and as the contract was in don Gabriel's possession, don Gabriel would have had to be appealed to. The licenciado, before he began to read, would first have asked don Gabriel what he was to read and whether don Gabriel would pay more to have it read than these lousy Indians, who squatted in their usual fashion in his outer office instead of sitting on chairs.

The boys might also, of course, have gone to a public authority and asked an official to read the contract to them; but then again, don Gabriel had the contract. He would have gone to the official with it and said, "Cómo estás, compadre? I have ten good round duros here for you. What's that you say? The muchachos want to know what's in the contract? I told them that when I paid them their advances. Now that they've drunk up the money, naturally they want to get out of the contract."

"Naturally, no wonder," the official would have said. "What do you want me to read out to them, then? Just tell me and I'll read what you like, and if the fellows make any noise about it, I'll put them where you'll find them when you want them."

Six of the boys attempted to escape. They were the ones who had come forward of their own accord. The rest, who had taken on the debts of their relations and future fathers-in-law, made no attempt at escape, because once they had undertaken the responsibility it would have been a betrayal of the trust their families reposed in them.

Of the six who escaped, one was shot. Two were captured

and mercilessly flogged, two perished in their flight through the jungle. They were never heard of again.

One got back to his native village. He was like a wild man, covered with blood, reduced to skin and bone and with lips parched and split with fever. He told them in the village where the boys had been taken.

15

Narciso was no longer chief when that happened. Another jefe had been elected by the family groups.

One day late in the afternoon a number of men went to Narciso's hut to talk to him. Narciso knew why the men had come and what they wanted to talk to him about.

It was known to every man in the place that Narciso, while he was still jefe, had received a cask of brandy from don Gabriel, the secretary. But not one of the men who had come to talk to Narciso made any suggestion whatever that the brandy had been a bribe. He was only asked whether he remembered don Gabriel's ever having given a single man of the village a glass of brandy without some particular motive.

Narciso said quietly, "I cannot remember a single case."

One of the men then asked Narciso to accompany them outside. Narciso stood up and, looking around his house, which was dimly lighted by a few pine splinters, went over to his youngest child, who was asleep on a petate on the ground. He touched its head, and after looking around the room once more, he followed the men out into the night.

Two hours later the men carried Narciso's body back to his house. He had been killed with a machete. It had happened out in the bush owing to a regrettable error when the men were clearing away the undergrowth in their search for a young mule which had apparently run away. Everyone in the place repeated this story. And everyone in the place knew what was behind it.

Narciso's wife and daughters began to wail. Immediately the hut was filled with all the women of their family group and of others who were friendly with them.

The body was put on a bier made of thin branches. Narciso's wife washed the blood from the face; and she washed the clotted blood from the hair and combed it.

Pine torches were brought and lighted. Then all the women squatted on the ground around the body, covered their heads with their rebozos or their jorongos, and began to bewail the dead.

16

The boy who had succeeded in reaching the village from the montería died four days later. He had been utterly exhausted and could not withstand his raging fever.

Two mounted guards in the service of the company who had been sent in pursuit of him found him on his bier in his father's hut. They insisted that the father or brother of the dead boy had to take over his debt because he had run away. When this was refused the guards informed them that the matter would be reported to the mayor of Hucutsín, who was responsible for the contract, and also to the jefe político of the district. The family would then find out what had to be done.

A secretary, who could have assisted them in capturing their prey, was not on the spot: Since don Gabriel's departure the jefe político had not found anybody who seemed to him suited to take over the post.

The place was left for more than two years without a secretary. The door of the prison was left to molder. The roof caved in over the office in the cabildo, where the table stood with the ink bottle on it and the pen with its rusty nib, and on which lay the piles of regulations concerning the well-being and education of the Indians.

As the Indians did not patch up the roof, more and more of

it broke away. The telephone wire was in order; even the instrument in the office was in order, until one day it was damaged by the falling roof. But there was no one there who took the trouble to telephone.

In spite of this, the sun was still in the sky. In spite of this, the maize grew in the fields. In spite of this, the Indian wives bore their husbands child after child. The people of the village managed perfectly well on their own. It never occurred to one of them that the place was in a desperate situation because no secretary was sent to govern it. Not one of them thought for a moment that the world might come to an end and mankind perish because they were not governed.

For this reason the idea came to none of them, not to the chief nor to any of the village council, to send a submissive report to the governor or the jefe político, reminding these gentry that the place lacked a secretario and in consequence had no means of communication with the central government.

Gerónimo, who was now chief, said one day when the men were assembled to decide upon the allotment of the common land among the new families, "I should like it best if the government forgot us for good. I have said all I have to say, my brothers and friends."

9

 As often happens in this world, where a good God controls all human destinies for the best and never makes a mistake, good luck was constantly on don Gabriel's side, while the innocent and the wretched had all the ill luck that could rattle down upon them from any direction and for any reason. This is a nice disposition of the Almighty which no man on earth has the right to criticize. For however incomprehensible a process may seem to men, the more certain it is that God in His great wisdom and eternal, inscrutable love for humanity has need of this incomprehensible process in order to pursue, through spiral mists of infinity, a definite aim known only to Himself.

It was owing to this quite sufficient cause that don Gabriel was pursued by good luck so persistently that there was no escape from it. Scarcely a day passed without his getting one more man contracted, and with every man he captured his fortune was increased by something between twenty-five and fifty-five pesos.

He did not take all those he bound by contract along with him. In that case he would have had them all at his heels from finca to finca and village to village. As soon as he got a man, he made the local secretary or the finquero or the chief of police answerable for the man's punctual arrival on the day of the festival of the Candelaria at Hucutsín, where all recruited labor was assembled before being marched off to the monterías from this outpost of civilization. Or, when don Gabriel and don Ramón decided to escort the men to the monterías themselves, they charged the local officials with seeing that the men arrived at a village or town on a certain date predesignated by them.

The local secretaries, the mayors, finqueros, or police officials received payment from the agent of the debts or fines on account of which the men were handed over. The agent had enough sense never to give the creditor payment of the whole sum due—only about a quarter of it was paid. This also made it possible for an agent to employ a smaller working capital. The balance was paid after the men had been delivered to the monterías. The agents by that time had their checks, which they cashed at Jovel or Tuxtla, and had plenty of money to settle up with.

In this way there was little risk of an agent's losing his money; and it seldom happened that a contract laborer did not turn up. If the man failed for any reason to leave his native place in time to arrive at Hucutsín on the proper day, he was guilty of breach of contract, the worst offense that an Indian laborer could commit under the dictatorship of don Porfirio. An Indian who had murdered one of his fellow men, that is to say another Indian—incurred a smaller penalty than for breach of contract.

It did not matter whether there was an Indian more or less in Mexico, or anywhere else on the American continent—they increased fast enough even though four-fifths of the children perished before they were twelve years old—but it did matter, and mattered more than all else, that the foreign companies, who exploited the wealth of the country, should always have enough labor. This was guaranteed by their concession grants and licenses. Breach of contract by an Indian laborer was high treason. Therefore going on strike was punished with death, because it was breach of contract on the part of, and together with, labor in general. A contract-breaking Indian lowered exports, and lowered exports were detrimental to the credit of the country. This had the effect of putting the country at the mercy of the foreigner, who is always the enemy, merely because he is a foreigner. Hence breach of contract by an Indian laborer was high treason.

And so if an Indian who had entered into a contract did not leave his native place on the appointed date, he was arrested by the police or the soldiers. The costs of taking him in charge were debited to him. If he was very fortunate and God took him under His wing, he got only fifty merciless lashes; if he made trouble, he got two hundred and fifty; and if the Holy Virgin had utterly forsaken him and took no account of him at all, five hundred.

There is no necessity, then, to explain in further detail why the agents felt no anxiety about the punctual appearance of their men when the lists were read out on the evening of the day they were all collected for the next morning's march into the jungle. If a man was absent, in ninety-nine cases out of a hundred it could be assumed that he was dead, or had lost an arm or a leg, and so was of no use to any montería and therefore of no use to his country.

2

Don Gabriel's invariable luck brought him to Pebvil at the very moment when he could net a good catch.

Pebvil was so independent and self-willed a place that don Gabriel had had doubts of getting even a single man there. Every attempt the Spaniards had made in the three hundred years of

Spanish rule to dissolve their pueblo and break it up into fincas had failed—the pueblo was too strong. When small groups and single families could not hold out, they gave way; but if a finquero settled on the land of these deflated Indian families, he was murdered or driven out as soon as the soldiers left. The Spaniards despaired of getting the pueblo under their yoke. Only a single concession could be extracted from the pueblo: the Indians accepted the presence of a secretario in Pebvil. But the Spanish governors, following the good advice of merchants and artisans of Spanish origin, finally reached the conclusion that it was more favorable to business in general and to peaceable and profitable trade to recognize the independence of the pueblo and to live in harmony with the members of the tribe, buying their products from them and selling them other goods in exchange. Both the Indian pueblo and the large Mexican town nearest to it, which was the pueblo's chief market, benefited greatly by this mutual and peaceful arrangement. It resulted in the pueblo's accounting for half the trade of the Mexican town.

Pebvil was a federation of four tribes who all spoke the same language, had the same customs and traditions, dressed in the same way, and were so closely allied that a young man of one tribe could marry into any of the other three, if a girl of another tribe pleased him and the wedding gift to her father was within his means.

About fifteen thousand independent Indians belonged to this federated nation. Their capital was given the same name, Pebvil, by which the whole nation was called. At the capital were the cabildo and a church. The secretary lived and carried on his duties in the cabildo. The pueblo, the federal community of family groups, was ruled by an Indian jefe.

The open space where the church and the cabildo stood and around which about thirty families lived was the political center of the nation. It was here the family groups assembled for the yearly festival and it was here the representatives of the tribes and family groups met in council.

From this center the different tribes radiated in four directions. Generally from three to ten families lived in one group. They were settled, according to the lay of the land and its fertility, from three hundred to more than a thousand paces apart in any direction.

The whole territory was divided according to the four points of the compass and all these groups of three or four or ten families belonged to the barrio, that is, to the district, of the north, the south, the east, or the west. Each barrio had its primitive Indian name, but under the influence of the Catholic religion, each of the old Indian names was prefaced by a pious one in order to limit the power and mischief of the devil. Thus one barrio was San Andrés, another San Marco, the next San Pedro, and the fourth San Miguel. Each of these barrios held a fiesta on the day of its patron saint.

Each barrio had from ancient times its own industry, which was respected by all the others. No barrio ever tried to enter the industry of another. One barrio made pots and earthenware, the second made hats, the third baskets and mats, and the fourth woolen blankets. No one from another barrio made his own hat. It was the invariable custom to buy a hat from the barrio which had the ancient privilege of making hats. In the same way no woman used a pot which had not been made in the barrio which had the right of making pots and plates for the whole people. And yet every Indian is capable of making his own hat, of weaving his own petate, of molding and firing his own cooking vessels.

There are almost as many systems of government among independent Indians as there are nations and languages. There are caciques who are elected for life, with the proviso that they can be set aside if they show themselves incapable; there are caciques who are not elected but who slowly ascend the ladder of office; there are regencies consisting not of one man but of four with equal rights and duties; there are casiques who are elected for four years, and others whose period of office lasts one year only; there are nations where a man who has once been casique can never again be elected to that office, however competent he may be; in other cases a casique can be re-elected after two, three, four, or more casiques have officiated since his last term. In some nations a man whose father has been casique can never himself be elected. However varied all these systems may be, they are all without exception of a republican and democratic nature.

Now, in Pebvil there was yet another system in force. If its origin could be successfully investigated it would certainly be found to lead back to that day when the nation migrated to this region in search of new territory. It must have settled down from the beginning in the four tribes which exist today. For political reasons and for better defense against other nations in their area the four tribes formed a federation, which assured to each tribe its independence.

To ensure to each of the four its rights and attributes and also to ensure the unity and strength of the federation, it was decided by a national council that the chief of the nation should be elected afresh each year. No one who had once been casique could be elected a second time. The barrios elected the casique in rotation. Only members of the barrio which was electing the casique for that year might vote. During his year of office the casique took up his abode in the capital of the federation, where he was allotted good land for himself and his family to cultivate. He was given no other payment or privilege for holding office. He was held responsible by the representatives of all four barrios for any mistakes in his administration.

The ceremony by which a new chieftain was instituted in his office was a remarkable one. In earlier times it had taken place on the sixth day after the shortest day—which according to our calendar would be about the twenty-seventh or twenty-eighth of December. Later the people began to hold it on New Year's Day.

At six o'clock in the morning all the members of the barrio that had elected the chief for the new year would march onto the open space in front of the cabildo, bringing the elected chief with them. The members of the other three barrios could also join in the ceremony.

A few men ran ahead to ring the church bells. There was no priest in the church. He made the extremely arduous journey to this isolated spot in high and mountainous country only once a year to scramble through a hurried Mass, to baptize children, to bless marriages already twenty years old in sinful delights, to sprinkle with holy water graves whose exact location could no longer be ascertained, to visit with the apostolic blessing all sheep, whether human or woolly, and to pocket the money for the Mass, the christenings, the blessings, the expenditure of holy water, and the forgiveness of unsanctified and unblessed marriages. The señor Cura did not appear at the festival of the institution of the new chief because on this day, New Year's Day, it paid better to work in the Lord's vineyard in the church of a large town.

While the bells pealed to celebrate the changeover from one chief to another, fireworks were set off to the accompaniment of music, dancing, frolic, and noise. Then the newly elected chief was introduced to the retiring chief and his council in front of the entrance to the cabildo by the assembled men of his tribe. With this introduction the result of the election was confirmed.

The retiring chief made a speech in the communal language. It was poetic in form and apparently of great antiquity. Then with much ceremony the staff of office was handed over.

The new chieftain replied politely and modestly. He too made use of the old rhymes which were appointed for this ceremony and which were probably a thousand years old or more.

Now a chair was brought up. It was a low chair woven of wickerlike twigs. The seat had a hole in the middle.

The new chieftain pulled down his white cotton trousers and sat on the chair, while all the men who had crowded around to watch the ceremony laughed and made ribald jokes.

Holding the ebony staff with its silver knob in his right hand, the chief sat solemnly in the chair, his face turned to all the men of his nation standing before him. He sat there with majestic dignity as though he were performing the first solemn act of his office. The laughing and joking of the crowd was stilled, to show that the first weighty utterance of their new chief was awaited with due respect.

But now three men came up, sent by the barrio which was to elect the casique for the following year. These men carried an earthenware pot with holes bored into its sides. The pot was filled with glowing charcoal, glowing brightly because of the holes.

One of the men explained in rhymed verses the purpose that the pot of fire would serve, and when he had concluded, he put this pot of glowing charcoal under the seat of the new chief.

He said in his speech that the fire under the chief's posterior was to remind him that he was not sitting on this seat to rest himself but to work for his people; he was to look alive even though he sat on the chair of office. Furthermore, he was not to forget who had put the fire under him—a member of the barrio that would appoint the chief for the next year—and that it was done to remind him from the outset that he could not cling to the office but had to give it up as soon as his time was up, so as to prevent any risk of a lifelong rule, which would be injurious to the welfare of his people. If he tried to cling to his office they would put a fire under him that would be large enough to consume both him and his chair.

As soon as the pot of glowing charcoal had been placed beneath the chair, rhymed sayings were recited, first by a man of the barrio of the retiring chief, next by a man of the barrio who would elect the chief for the following year, and last by a man of the barrio of the newly appointed chief.

The new chief had to remain seated until these recitals were at an end. It depended on his popularity with the people whether the men who recited these sayings chanted them in slow and measured tones or as fast as they possibly could without openly giving the show away. If the last man to recite thought the two who spoke before him had recited too quickly, he would make up for it by reciting his verses twice as slowly.

Whatever the chief might feel, he would not show by even a movement or the flicker of an eyelid how hot it was for him. Quite the opposite. When the sayings had all been recited he did not jump up at once in relief that his warming was over, but remained sitting for a good while to show that he had no intention of running away from the pains and troubles which his office might hold in store for him. Very often he made this the occasion for a joke, which increased the good humor of the men who watched eagerly to see whether a sign of discomfort might escape him and give them an opportunity of laughing at him. The more cheerful his jokes and the longer he remained seated the more respect and confidence he won from the men.

He tried by his jokes to turn the laugh against them. "You have no lungs, you weaklings," he might say. "What will your wives say to you if you are too weak to blow up the fire underneath my behind? There is no warmth at all coming up through the hole. Here you, Eliseo, come here and scrape off the ice that is forming on my buttocks."

When the charcoal died down the chief got up slowly. The ice he had spoken of had not been so innocent. Great blisters had been raised on his skin and in places it was so well roasted that it could be smelled from a distance.

A friend came up and smeared his backside with oil and then applied a compress of crushed herbs, while another poured him a huge glassful of tequila.

The new chief would not forget for weeks what he had had under his seat. It helped him considerably during his period in office to carry out his duties as his nation had expected of him when it elected him.

In nearly all cases scars were left on the exposed parts, which proved to his last days better than any moldering document that he had once had the honor of being chief of his nation. They also made it certain that he would never think of being elected a second time against the practice of the people.

Workers would be advised to adopt this well-proven Indian method of election, particularly with the officials of their trade unions and political organizations—and not only in Russia, where it is most necessary. In all other countries, too, where Marx and Lenin are set up as saints the militant working class could achieve success much more surely if they lit a good fire yearly under their leaders' behinds. No leader is indispensable. And the more often leaders are put on red-hot seats, the more lively the political movement would be. Above all things, the people must never be sentimental.

3

Don Porfirio Díaz had himself re-elected every four years when his time as president was up. The gang who waxed fatter and fatter under his regency did the electing. Whoever did not wax fat under his government had no vote. What he had needed was a brazier under his backside the first time he was elected to remind him that there is more than one man on earth who is capable of ruling a people's destiny; that, in fact, every tenth man in every nation is capable of governing. There is nothing mysterious about it. It is much more difficult to construct a machine which will work than to rule a people where the machinery is already there and in going order. The art of governing is only made out to be mysterious in order to frighten revolutionaries and to prevent the simple subject from knowing how little capacity and knowledge is needed for government. How many half-wits and idiots have governed their peoples for half a century in peace and glory!

Don Porfirio considered himself the best and greatest and most intelligent statesman on earth. Hence he considered that it went without saying that he should be elected again and again. And everyone below him followed his example. Governors, mayors, police chiefs, secretaries, and engineers remained in office until death relieved the people of them. If they fell into dotage or idiocy, that was no proper reason why they should be retired. They would have demanded pensions. It was better for the finances of the country to leave them in office until they could be buried than to pay salaries twice over, once to the pensioned and again to those in office.

4

Amalio was the casique of the Pebvil Indians. He was the elected jefe of the barrio San Andrés.

Amalio was a drunkard. Another failing he had was that he allowed himself to be influenced by don Abelardo, the secretario. Don Abelardo had contrived little by little to bring the chief entirely over to his side. He had promised him that if he worked well with the government the governor of the state would give him a large piece of the best land, which would be taken away from a hacienda that bordered the Indian territory on the west.

The secretary put his proposals very cleverly. He knew that the jefe of the Indians would not betray or sell out his people. If, however, by working well with the government he could win a large piece of good land for his nation, it would be to his nation's advantage. He would settle on the new land with his family and then the land he was occupying would be free for a new family.

Don Abelardo advised the casique to say nothing about these proposals in the pueblo so that no unnecessary excitement would be aroused. It might happen, he said, that the governor would decide on a different piece of land, perhaps to the east of the Indian territory, and then the people, if they had already counted on this new land's being to the west, would think they had been taken advantage of. This would only give rise to a lot of talk and discussion which would do no good to anybody. Although the reason given by the secretario had only a vague connection with the matter in hand, the chief thought the secretary did well to advise him to say nothing to the people about the proposal.

The chief, according to the design laid out to him by the secretary, was to work well with the government, but by that the secretary meant that the Indian should work well with him, since he was the government there; at least, he regarded himself as the government.

When the working class works well with the capitalists and the middle-class political parties, it has always meant for hundreds of years that the worker pays the costs of the good understanding. It is just the same with the Indians. When they work well with the officials they are skinned for it.

5

With the help of the casique, who was not intelligent enough to see through the tactics of the secretary and who also was of weak character and could not resist brandy when he saw it in front of him, the secretary succeeded in greatly extending his influence. He allowed the governor, the state government, and the federal government an ample share of the proceeds; for the more he allowed them the less did anyone think of investigating his official activities.

The governor received complaint after complaint about the secretary's unscrupulous administration—there were charges of unjust taxation, charges of confiscating animals or produce which the Indians intended to take to market but which were taken from them by the secretary in payment of taxes or fines, of whose existence they first heard through the confiscation. Whole gangs of men were levied to work by compulsion on roads and public buildings without receiving either wages or food. The wages allowed for the labor of the Indians appeared in the accounts of the state or federal government and in the budgets and were paid for by taxation, but the money was shared by the governor, the government engineer in charge, and the secretario who produced the men.

When in the neighboring Mexican town a manufacturer wanted hands, or when a trader was transporting goods through the country and wanted to spare himself the expense of pack mules, they sent messages to the secretary, who the next morning sent them the required number of men.

The manufacturers got the laborers and the traders the boys who took on the work of pack mules, and the secretary pocketed the wages of the men he dispatched, while the Indians, free citizens of the Republic, had to take even their food with them.

The secretary could not do all this on his own. He had no power to command these independent Indians. The power of command was in the hands of the Indian jefe, who alone could issue direct commands to his people. This was very clever of the government; for if it had issued commands to this nation of Indians more soldiers would have been needed to suppress rebellions than the government could ever have paid the war office for.

The secretary always had regulations of some kind on hand

to show why the Indians had to produce so many men for public works: because the government respected their communal land—instead of confiscating it; because it allowed the Indians to use the state roads to take their produce and cattle to market—and there pay the appointed tax on every sale; because it did not forbid them to hold festivals in their own territory; because it allowed them to drink brandy—and to pay for it; and because it did not even think of depriving them of the rights to fish and hunt game within their own boundaries.

All these rights, which the Indians had possessed in any case as long as American soil existed, had to be expressly purchased afresh from the government every day and freshly ratified. Otherwise there would be no need of a government.

The Indian jefe obeyed the regulations of the government, and obeyed them in the form in which the secretario, who could read and write, chose to expound and interpret them.

6

Quite often the Indians had extremely intelligent and quick-witted men as their jefes, men who were such good diplomats that without openly opposing the government they continued to be very sparing of the labor and money which they yielded to it. During their periods of office their nation increased in prosperity, and ruthless exploitation and injustices were hard to put into execution.

The jefes had to be good diplomats. They had always to face three ways: there was the government, the secretary, and their own people. When it came to the art of government, the jefe of a large independent Indian nation in a situation like this had to be ten times more diplomatic and adroit than the man who was at the head of the Mexican Republic. The jefe was not excused by his people when he made mistakes: he was answerable for each one. It was his duty to hold the balance among the three parties. He had to see that the people were not harried and robbed, and that not a reproach could be made against him for having at any moment neglected their advantage. But in refusing the demands of the government, he could not go too far; otherwise a battalion of soldiers would be quartered in the place and in a few months the pueblo would be so pillaged that not a sheep or a goat would be found on the pastures—for when soldiers are quartered on an Indian pueblo they pay nothing for what they consume or waste for their pleasure. The jefe would be made answerable for the arrival of soldiers, because he ought not to have let things get so out of hand.

7

It is therefore quite understandable that don Abelardo, when he had been blessed with so feeble and slow-witted a jefe as Amalio, would exert all his influence to keep him in office until he had filled his pockets and could give up his post as secretary.

The present jefe had made himself thoroughly unpopular with his people. The whole nation was only waiting for a new man to represent them in the cabildo; and just because the man who was most likely to be elected by his barrio was the direct opposite of Amalio, it was as good as certain that he would be elected. If for no other reason, it would be done to annoy the secretario, for every child knew that there was no one the secretary hated so much as this man whose election seemed certain.

Don Abelardo was afraid of this man because he knew him to be a forthright, sagacious, and self-willed man, who would make it almost impossible for him to get what he wanted.

So don Abelardo began to take earnest measures to keep in office a jefe with whom he got on so well. He wrote a long report to the governor, expressing his view of the system of yearly election which was the practice in Pebvil. He said outright that it was nonsense; for as soon as a jefe had got into the saddle and was just beginning to reap the benefits of his experience, he had to give up his office because another jefe had been elected.

What the secretary said was nothing new. The same thing has been said for thousands of years. It is the reason why there are hereditary kings, why there are presidents and deputies elected for life, and why there are dictators. The officials of labor organizations, too, who do not want to take a back seat though the time has come around ten times over, fall back on the same argument.

The report made a deep impression on the governor. He saw at once that the system was not favorable to a stable, conservative regime. There was the danger that such a system might be taken as a pattern; and if you were to have a new president and a new governor every year, the people might come to believe that one person could govern as well as another, for in twenty years you would have twenty regents and all of them knowing how to govern. From this it might appear that ruling was not so difficult as the ruled were made to believe.

Besides this, the governor was a man who wanted to keep his office forever, because it was comfortable and brought in business as nothing else could. And then at the top, at the very head of the nation, was a man who did not mean to get off his chair, however the chair might be shaken and pushed about.

As don Porfirio intended to sit there for life and as the governor, too, hoped to be a lifelong governor, the governor declared the system in vogue at Pebvil a stupidity and a proof that nothing good could be expected of Indians, who were still sunk in barbarism. He commanded by decree that the present jefe, Amalio, had either to be elected again, or else to remain in office by virtue of the last election.

Don Abelardo read out the decree in the presence of Amalio and a few Indians who happened to be in the cabildo.

It was not easy to make out whether the jefe was pleased by

this decree or not. He said, "If that is the government's command, we can only fall into line."

"No question about it," don Abelardo threw in. "Orders are orders. You remain jefe, don Amalio. There is no more to be said."

The other Indians who were present said nothing. They listened quietly without a movement or any change of expression.

It was November when that happened.

8

On the morning of the last day of the second week after the arrival of this decree, a deputation from the San Miguel barrio came to the cabildo to speak with the secretario. San Miguel was the district whose turn it was to elect the jefe for the following year.

Natividad, the man whose election was certain, was not in the deputation. The men who composed it, seven in number, were ordinary Indians to look at—small peasants. They wore sandals on their naked feet. They had spotlessly clean white cotton shirts and trousers on. These articles of clothing were in some cases so patched that not a piece of the original cloth appeared to have survived. All carried their jorongos—their ponchos of gray wool with a long fringe at each end—thrown over their shoulders. Their trousers were pulled up high above the knee according to the custom of their nation; and their muscular calves and legs looked as if they had been carved out of old hardwood, like those wooden statues of Christ which are centuries old.

The men took their hats off as soon as they entered the office. Each one in turn stepped up to the secretary, told him his name and touched his hand with his fingertips, and with a bow stepped back to his place. Don Abelardo offered them cigarettes. Each took one and began to smoke. Then the secretary asked whether they would not like to sit on the bench. They replied that they preferred to stand.

All of them had brought their machetes and three their shot-guns, the ordinary Spanish muzzle-loaders, but they had left their weapons outside in the portico of the cabildo. Two men who had come with them squatted on the trodden earth of the portico smoking and talking. The dogs that had accompanied this delegation chased each other on the open space in front of the cabildo and quarreled and played with the dogs of the place.

9

After the men in the office had smoked for a time the secre-tario asked them, "Qué puedo hacerle?" What could he do for them?

One of the Indians stepped forward. He was called Tomás and had been appointed spokesman for the deputation.

"We have heard that a decree has been made for our co-marca."

"That is true," said don Abelardo.

"We have the right to know what this decree for our terri-tory says."

"You have the right," replied the secretary. "The decree of the governor in Tuxtla declares that the system of election used in your nation is null and void."

"Neither the governor nor the federal government of the Republic of Mexico," replied Tomás, "can set aside the system of election which holds good for our comarca without first obtaining our consent. Our customs bind us alone—we do not force the Ladinos or any other Indian nation to follow our practices and customs. For this reason we allow nobody, not even the president of the Republic, the right to force upon us customs whose usefulness we have not tested and of which we do not see the benefit for our people. We have no objection to looking into the advantages and disadvantages of a new way of voting and to testing its usefulness, but we cannot and will not permit the government to interfere with rights which concern our own comarca only."

Tomás did not say this fluently and all at one go. He said it slowly and very deliberately and spoke in halting Spanish. Sometimes he spoke a few words first in his own language so as to make his thoughts clear to himself and to let his companions, only two of whom spoke Spanish, understand what he was saying.

The secretary understood the language spoken in Pebvil, although he could only speak it with difficulty. He sat at the table with his legs crossed and listened with composure. Then he lit another cigarette and handed the package around, but not one of the men took any.

"It is a government decree," he said at last. "I can do nothing at all about it. I did not ask for the decree."

The men knew from long experience that no decision, least of all a decree touching on the affairs of an Indian nation, would be made without the secretario's being asked for his advice and comments. The secretary is the middleman between the Indian nation, to which he has been appointed secretary, and the government. A decision would scarcely, if ever, be reached, unless the secretary who lived with the Indians and knew their customs, as well as their peculiarities and tendencies, had given it his blessing, or at least had given no warning.

Knowing this, the men took the word of the secretario for what it was worth. They did not say that he could easily have prevented the decree if he had wished. They made no criticism either of his conduct or the government's.

Tomás, the spokesman, said, "We have come to say that we do not consider that the decree exists for us. We shall elect our jefe as we have always done; and for our nation no one is jefe unless we have elected him. We have nothing to do with a jefe whom we have not elected or whose term is over. You will soon find out whether you or the government can do anything with our nation with the help of a man whom we do not recognize as our jefe."

"The decree is not in the least meant to injure the great and noble nation of Pebvil," the secretary said. "Amalio is an excellent jefe. He has learned a great deal by working with me in the cabildo. A new jefe will have to learn everything from the beginning before he understands it all and can be of real use to you."

To this Tomás said, "It is not our business to decide whether Amalio is a good or a bad jefe for us and that is not why we have come. Suppose him to be an excellent jefe, the best we have had for dozens of years. That is no reason why we should alter our ancient customs in one day. It might easily happen that another jefe would not be so good as Amalio and we would not be able to get rid of him when we wanted."

"The Republic of Mexico is a thousand times greater than Pebvil," said don Abelardo, "and in this great Republic of Mexico don Porfirio has been jefe now for thirty-two years. He has always been re-elected time after time, and it has turned out very well. Year by year he has enriched his experience and been able to make use of it for the good of the people. The governor of this state has also been re-elected time after time, just as the governors of the other federated states have been too."

Tomás waited politely in case the secretary wished to add anything more, but when don Abelardo remained silent, the Indian said, "That is no doubt the right and necessary thing for the Ladinos, but that is just why it may be very far from the best thing for us Tsotsils. We have existed for thousands of years and we have not gone under, although we have different customs and different systems of government than those of the Ladinos. And as we have lived for thousands of years with our own customs and thrived without needing the Ladinos or asking their advice and adopting their manners and summoning them to our country, we are sure that our customs are no worse than those of the Ladinos. We have lived for thousands of years in this manner, just as we thought good and right for ourselves, and we have convinced ourselves that we can live with this system and these customs of ours for thousands of years longer without going to pieces or being overcome. We have found through age-long experience that it suits our people to choose a new jefe every year, to take him every year from a different barrio, and never to re-elect a man who has once been jefe. If we were engaged in a long war and wanted the most experienced man as jefe, or if we were on a long migration to new territory, then it might be advisable to keep the most experienced man among us in office for a longer time. But the tradition of our people tells us that we have not altered our method of election even in critical times. Never once in our long history has a jefe held office for longer than one year. If the new jefe lacks knowledge and experience, he can get help and advice and support on all sides from previous jefes who have more experience than he has. There is not a man among us, whether he is jefe or not, whether he has been or whether he will be, who will not put all his knowledge and experience at the service of our nation if the people have need of his advice and help. That is why we have never had kings and dictators and despots. Every man, even the simplest, can be made jefe for a year if he has or can win the confidence of the grown men of his barrio. We have often had, and I know this from the stories of my grandfather, a jefe who was so clever and so competent that everyone would have been glad if he had held office longer and been able to carry out his plans. But it has usually happened that the next jefe has been even better than the last; for everyone learns from his predecessor, and each new jefe has the ambition to show greater zeal and capacity than the man before him and to earn even greater praise. The more often a new man can be chosen as jefe the more of our people can be jefe, and the more of us learn how to govern. The more men know of how to govern, the better they are in council. Our desire is that every one of us should be a jefe once. Then we criticize less, but we advise better. The men of the people constitute a parliament of regents. Men who have once been jefe are better citizens because they have learned how important it is to obey on occasions when the welfare of the nation is at stake. But the most important asset is that since every person brings at least one idea into the world that no one has had before him, every new jefe brings an idea to the administration of our people and has the chance to prove whether it is any good or not. Everyone believes that he can do everything better than anyone else if only he were in office. We give all our citizens a chance to show whether they can do better than others. Everybody who has once held office has learned that maize must be boiled or roasted if it is to be eaten and digested. That is what I was sent here to say on behalf of my people. We do not criticize the government of the Ladinos, but we give no one on earth, who does not belong to our people, the right to alter our manners and customs as he deems fit. If the government could convince us that our system is harmful to us, we would consider the matter and do what we thought best. The great drawback of the system the government wishes to impose upon us is that if a man who has been chosen jefe betrays the trust of those who chose him and is not what the people expected of him, he cannot be put aside, or only with great difficulty. Even if he is a rogue, who looks out for himself rather than for his people, or is domineering, egoistic, and vainglorious, still he will try by intrigues and by poisoning the minds of the people to remain in office. This is bound to lead to corruption, to unrest and rebellions. We, however, wish to live in peace among ourselves and with our neighbors, because we have learned after thousands of years that only peace and harmony bring us prosperity."

10

It is not to be supposed that the secretary understood all that the Indian meant. Partly this was because he did not pay much attention. In his view the decree was a fact, and these lousy Indians had no right to object—they were merely subjects. They had to obey and to do whatever their dictators saw fit to command. Another reason why he did not understand was that the Indian belonged to a world and a way of looking at things which were as remote from him as the notes of the trumpet call to the last judgment.

But one thing the secretary had understood. Tomás had managed his speech very cleverly. He had carefully and deliberately kept until the end the particular case which the secretary had made use of to get this decree passed.

Amalio had not been mentioned by name in the peroration. Nevertheless, don Abelardo had understood at once who was meant. And though his peroration was full of merciless digs at the secretary, it had been so well thought out by the Indian that don Abelardo could not say he had been insulted, or been accused of corrupting and dividing the Indian nation for his personal advantage.

He found himself quite unable to make any reply. He would not have known where to start. The Indian had armed himself with those thousand or ten thousand years during which his nation had evolved and practiced this system of government, probably after long continued dissensions which threatened to destroy the people. It was impossible to argue against results which had their roots in a thousand years of experience. He did not even venture an attempt to make objections, because he felt sure the Indian would score him. So he only said, "A decree is a decree, Tomás; you have got to obey it. You can tell your people that. Amalio is going to remain jefe for another year, and whether he will still be jefe the year after that will be settled when the time comes."

"I will report what you say to the men of Pebvil," said Tomás quietly. "I have no authority to make any further reply to what you say, don Abelardo."

He approached the table. The secretary got up and went around the table to meet him. Tomás touched the fingertips of the secretary's outstretched hand and said, "Adiós, señor." Then with a deep bow he left the office.

The other men of the deputation likewise took their leave and followed their spokesman. They picked up their machetes in the portico, threw their shotguns over their shoulders, and marched off. They said not a word to one another.

11

The whole nation knew that the deputation had been with the secretario, but not a man in Pebvil, along whose maguey fences the deputation now went on their way home to their barrio, came up to ask about the result of the interview with the secretario.

This might perhaps be taken as a lack of interest on the part of the Indians. A case like this, however, arouses nothing that you can call interest in an Indian. He knows what is happening and what has to happen. More than this he does not need to know. Every member of the nation knew long before the deputation was sent that the negotiation with the secretario was in reality no negotiation, no attempt to make a compromise, no balancing of parliamentary parties. The discussion with the secretary was the final warning, nothing more.

Yet it was not a declaration of war. The nation did not desire war either with the government or with the Ladinos. They were not so foolish as to come out with machetes and shotguns against machine guns and mountain artillery. This is only done by civilized peoples when they want to lose two million of their best men and enslave themselves to debt for six hundred years.

The uncivilized Indians, who could not read and write and who were therefore less easily led into folly, never thought of bringing such danger on their people and wasting its wealth and manhood. They were a people of governors and had neither a war department nor steel manufacturers nor armament firms.

Since they were a people of governors with plenty of men who had learned by short periods of office to give good advice and to judge the advice given by others, they could not be stampeded by a horde of fanatics until all fell into the same pit. They acted like barbarian Indians; but they acted rightly, successfully, and inexorably. And punctually.

12

The first of January had come. A thick morning mist hung over the earth, which was bathed in dew.

As day dawned over Pebvil and the mist unwillingly broke up and drifted away and the sun topped the mountain in one leap, thousands upon thousands of Indians filled the square.

This mass of people appeared as suddenly as if they had spent the night hidden among the bushes, waiting for the sun to send its first flicker of light over the crest of the mountain. Indeed, they filled the whole open space so swiftly and so evenly that it seemed they had been lying in wait between the blades of grass and in the crevices of the earth and then risen to their feet as one man.

There was a murmur such as was heard only on this day, the day of their nation's most important ceremony. Men and women and children and dogs were gathered in small, tight groups and in larger, looser assemblages. All were in high spirits. There was laughing, shouting, joking, calling, singing, and music-making all over the wide space.

Some of the men of the tribes had long staves with brightly colored feathers at the top, and these were planted like banners in the center of each group. Others had come with flags on which Saint Anthony or the Virgin was clumsily stitched.

Here and there among the crowd the captains could be distinguished by the variously colored silk ribbons fluttering from their hats. The captains, too, were elected yearly. They were elected by their tribes as representatives to the great council presided over by the chief of the nation. Now, at this gathering of the whole nation on this extraordinary occasion, they were the leaders and marshals of their tribes. By means of them each tribe was in close and constant touch with the central council of the whole nation. At the last decisive meeting all the captains had been instructed on what their tribes were to do in given events and at given moments and on how and where they were to lead them at given signals from the central council.

Don Abelardo, the secretary, was greatly astonished to see the whole nation assembled on the square in front of the cabildo so early in the morning. He could think of no ready explanation. It was not the saint's day of any of the four barrios, but since he did not know all the feast days and other occasions on which the nation assembled, he was not alarmed.

Then it occurred to him that it was the first of January, and he supposed they must have come to celebrate the new year. He was not aware that Indians do not celebrate the new year. Taking this to be the explanation, he went in to breakfast.

When he emerged again onto the portico he asked some Indians who were standing nearby talking to one another what the reason for the mass assembly was. They replied with remarkable alacrity that it was the first of January. Don Abelardo was reassured.

13

He sent out the police—Indians who lived at Pebvil—to keep order. While he stood there wondering what else he could do to show that he was in authority, the church bells began to peal. Looking across, he saw that the low belfry was occupied by a crowd of young men who were shouting, yelling, and screaming as they wildly swung the wheels of the bell cage.

Then, from the bush on one side of the square a crowd of Indians came marching to the sound of music. They had drums, flutes, guitars, and violins, and played dance tunes. They carried staves adorned with flowers and feathers. In front of the column the church banners of their barrio were borne aloft by some youths with all the dignity they could muster.

The secretary knew by the flags that this marching column was the barrio of San Miguel. Its arrival was greeted with wild excitement and shouts of welcome, and numbers of young men ran out to escort the newcomers to the square.

The captains of the barrio could be seen just behind the banners, and among them marched Natividad, the man whom the barrio San Miguel had elected as chief. Natividad's hat had no streamers—it was part of the ceremony of installing him to tie the streamers on—but he wore two bright sashes across his chest and these singled him out as chief-elect.

The column had scarcely reached the edge of the square when Amalio, who by decree was to remain in office, came running at great speed to the cabildo. He pushed open the door of the office, shouting back to the secretary, "They're here, they're here. Me matarán."

"Nonsense, estas loco," said don Abelardo, following him in. "Don't be crazy, no one will kill you. You are under the government's protection."

But the secretary did not appear to be so calm and confident as his words were meant to suggest. His face was ashen and he kept pulling at his belt to bring his revolver around. He looked down and counted the cartridges in the belt. He felt better when he saw that it was full to the last loop, forty-five of them, each bullet flattened and filed. The flattening was to smash the bones, and the filing to harbor dirt and microbes in the indentations so that even a flesh wound would prove fatal.

As soon as he had seen the Indian rush by with terror on his face—an unusual sight in an Indian—he knew in a flash the meaning of this gathering of thousands of people.

However he did not yet grasp the full seriousness of it. He thought that as secretary and as representative of the government he was strong enough to control the threatening situation by virtue of his authority.

14

Amalio knew better. He knew the customs of his race, and he felt no security in the office. He went out onto the portico and looked about for some way of escape, but the Indians were massed in a crescent as dense as a thick forest.

They were too far away for him to distinguish one man from another, but he could feel their pitiless hostility directed upon him. This huge gathering had one eye, and this one eye was fixed upon him in an unalterable and merciless resolve.

Don Abelardo came to the door. "Don Amalio," he said, "you have nothing to fear. You are to remain in office by the decree of the government, by its special command. I shall telephone to the garrison for a squadron of cavalry with machine guns. Go up into the schoolroom. You'll be safer there than here. Meanwhile the soldiers will be on the way."

The casique could not set himself against the orders of the government. That would have laid him open to the charge of disobedience and landed him in prison for years to come. It might even have gone worse than that with him, for the judge might have found that disobedience to a special decree of the governor was an act of rebellion and an open defiance of the power of the State, and in that case he would have been shot. He had neglected to seize the opportunity of declining a further tenure of office—on the plea that he was no longer fit for it—the day the decree arrived.

Besides, the obstinacy of his Indian character and his honor as a man forbade him to yield and confess himself beaten at the moment when danger threatened. Such conduct would so utterly have disgraced him in the eyes of his tribe and nation that he would have been driven out—to take to the jungle and starve there or be devoured by jaguars. He was in a position from which there was no retreat. His only hope lay in putting off his fate until the soldiers came and protected him.

15

The upper floor of the cabildo was reached by wooden steps at the eastern end of the building which led onto a balcony with a railing. Off this balcony was the schoolroom, which also served as sleeping quarters at night for passing travelers and traders. The schoolroom had no windows. It was lighted through the open door.

Amalio left the portico and went around the corner of the building to the steps in full view of all the thousands in the square. His wife saw him too, as he went up the steps. She knew instinctively that he was going to the upper floor because he no longer felt safe below, and from this she realized that these were perhaps the last steps her husband would take of his own free will.

She ran to her hut and got a jug of water, a few tortillas and chiles, some frijoles wrapped in banana leaves, and, gathering her four children, hastened back to the cabildo.

She made straight for the steps, hustling her children up them in front of her, while she put down her jug and provisions on the lowest step in order to tie the cloth, which held her unweaned baby on her back, more tightly across her chest.

The knot had loosened as she ran. Then she snatched up her load again and followed her children into the schoolroom.

Not one among all those thousands through whom she had had to make her way had spoken to her or stopped her. A lane had opened in front of her. Only they could say whether it was to avoid touching her or because they wished to speed her flight.

16

The column escorting the newly elected chief meanwhile marched merrily toward the cabildo. It went its way apparently without a care and without showing any sign of awareness of what was occurring in the cabildo. It was as though not a man among them had ever heard of the decree; for they advanced exactly as every barrio had for hundreds of years when a new chieftain was being installed, and they followed every ancient rite with ceremonious precision. As they could see nothing in what they did that threatened harm to any one of their own or any other people, it would have been impossible to convince them that they were guilty of rebellion or any unlawful act. They did not interfere in the political customs of the Mexicans and they did not therefore see why it was rebellion if they did not allow the Mexicans to interfere in theirs and to alter them by force to suit themselves.

Without the sounding of a signal or the waving of a flag the confused uproar of voices and instruments in the crowd suddenly ceased. A silence of suspense came down on all those thousands of Indians and filled the whole square. If a baby in arms here and there uttered a cry it was instantly stilled by its mother, and if a dog yelped it broke off into a whine at a kick from its master.

Only the column escorting the new chief marched on toward its goal as before, with music and singing and cheerful noise. Flags, some with the Mexican colors and the Mexican eagle, others with likenesses of the Virgin and the saints stitched on them, were waved about with shouts of encouragement. At the head of the column and on both sides of it were men with green scarves who, instead of marching, danced along, gesticulating and singing to a monotonous chant. Some of them wore fearsome masks—the jowls of jaguars or demons with the horns of oxen above. These marshals of the procession carried whips which they cracked in pretended anger. Without a word from them the massed crowds opened in a wide lane.

17

It was customary for the office of chief to be handed over in the front portico of the cabildo, from which one entered the secretary's office. It was not that the secretary had any part in the ancient ceremony of the Indians. He was merely an onlooker, and all he had to do was to note the name of the new chief and forward it to the government for its formal approval.

On this occasion, however, the procession marched to that end of the cabildo where the steps led up to the schoolroom. At this there was a movement in the crowd on the square. Most of the people had taken up positions facing the front of the cabildo. Now the whole crowd shifted to the east in order to have a better view of the ceremony.

This shifting of the whole crowd took place without any commotion or shouting. It was done in silence, and it seemed to don Abelardo, who had already bolted and barred all the doors and was watching through the cracks in them, so menacing that he took down his saddle harness with the intention of making his escape. He went to the kitchen and told his wife, who was rocking her youngest child on her knee, to get ready; it would be better, he said, if they cleared out while there was time. He sent his ten-year-old son out to find the horses and bring them in.

As don Abelardo watched, he could see some Indian boys

calling their fathers' attention to someone who had left the house and was running toward the prairie. It was don Abelardo's son. But the men paid no attention and did not even turn their heads in the direction in which the boys pointed. By this don Abelardo knew that no one took any heed of him; he, and still more his family, were safe.

He had been trying for half an hour to get the garrison at Jovel on the telephone. Now he heard some sounds coming through. This showed that the Indians had not cut the wires and confirmed his belief that they were not in open rebellion against the government.

18

The telephone wires in these remote regions are in such a state of neglect and disorder that for miles you find the wires lying on the ground. They are not fastened to special posts except when crossing bare and treeless plains, in which case the posts are trees hacked down in the nearest stretch of bush. They are misshapen, warped, bent, and distorted, as trees in the bush always are. The bark is left on. It would have taken too much time to remove it. They are driven into the ground as they are; and since they are not scraped or treated in any way they sometimes strike root and grow. Often there are no insulators, and if there are, they are broken. In these cases the wire is simply wound around the trunk. Since these posts are driven in with the least possible trouble, half of them fall in the first strong wind and the wire is left lying on the ground.

When the telephone wires traverse bush and wooded country there are no posts whatever. The wire is simply fastened to the trees, with insulators or without, according to the supply of them and the whim of the mechanics employed.

The toughest trees are sometimes uprooted or snapped in the terrible hurricanes which sweep over these tropical regions; and since hurricanes do not as a rule care whether people have the telephone or not, disaster may befall a tree to which the wire is attached, or it may as it falls tear the wire down from other trees and crush it against the ground on wet scrub.

Indians who happen to come across the wire lying on the ground might of course take it up and fasten it to a tree again; and would, no doubt, from the desire to be of help but for the risk of being shot on the spot by any official or military patrol if they were discovered tampering with the wire, no matter what explanation they gave. Since every Indian knows this, he gives any stretch of broken-down wire a wide berth.

There are also farmers and owners of haciendas passing by on horseback, educated people who know the value of the telephone to the authorities and to themselves, too, in cases of sickness when they want to summon the doctor. But they would never bother to get off their horses to lift the wire from the ground. If they have a boy with them they might perhaps tell him to hitch it up over the nearest green bush. In most cases, however, they would not let their boys stop to do it; they would say to themselves "What does it matter to me? I have other things to think about."

It requires, therefore, a felicitous conjunction of a number of coincidences before a secretary can hope to have the use of the telephone when he needs it. He scarcely ever gets through until the whole matter he had to talk about has been settled by an exchange of messages by hand. Often a secretary will sit the whole day long at the instrument waiting for the happy moment when all the trees and bushes are bone-dry. Getting through in the early morning when there is a heavy dew on tree and bush and grass would be considered so miraculous an occurrence that the secretary would talk of it for the rest of his life.

Why that distant state should institute and maintain a telephone service at all and at the same time be so oblivious of the elementary principles of keeping it in running order, would be wholly and utterly incomprehensible unless one knew the leitmotif of the piece. The state desires to be accounted civilized and so it announces in its statistics that it has so many thousand kilometers of telephone wires. It has them and even a few hundred more, but they can only be used when they are in the right mood.

Don Abelardo banked on midday when the dew would have evaporated; then if no rain fell he might be able to ask Jovel what he was to do, or what he could do, with these thousands of Indians camped on the plaza.

19

The sun had risen and stood with its chin on the edge of a near range of hills which bounded the mountain valley on the east. And now the procession escorting the newly elected chief reached that side of the cabildo where the steps led up to the schoolroom.

The low chair of state with the hole in the middle and all else required for the ceremony had been brought along in the procession. An Indian brought up the earthenware brazier and blew up the charcoal.

Now the men who carried the long staves adorned with brightly colored feathers formed a half circle. The captains stepped forward, repeated some verses, and then called to Natividad. The newly elected chief stepped into the half circle. The captains summoned the men with the church banners and the flags of the country, and Natividad knelt down. Each flag bearer in turn stepped up to the kneeling Natividad and waved his flag before him three times, and then Natividad touched the corner of the flag and kissed it. The captains after each kiss made three crosses in the air above Natividad's head and recited verses.

These sayings which accompanied the crosses in the air over Natividad's head were taken from Catholic ceremonies, or at least were liberally sprinkled with fragments of prayers; for among the Indian words could be heard *María, ave, pro nobis,* and other scraps of Latin.

Now the senior captain of San Miguel, who was the acknowledged master of ceremonies, stepped forward. He wore a sash across his chest and gay ribbons on his hat. In his right hand was a long staff with brightly colored feathers at its tip.

In a speech delivered in a singsong he called upon Amalio as the retiring chief to come forward to be greeted by and to greet the new chief and to hand over to him the staff of office.

It was the custom for the retiring chief to appear with the staff of office in his right hand while this speech was being made. As soon as the speech ended he had to reply. He greeted the senior captain, likewise in rhymed verses, then the other captains, and finally all the men, thanking them for the honor they had done him by turning to him in so grave a matter.

Next he greeted the new chief and said that it was a high honor to be permitted to hand over his office to so worthy a successor, whose honor and wisdom, whose courage and knowledge of affairs were well known to every man in every barrio of their noble nation. He added that his own powers were too feeble for him to have done all the nation had expected of him, although he had done his utmost to be just to all; but he hoped that his worthy and esteemed successor in the office which he now laid down in accordance with the custom of their people would fill it much better and more successfully than he himself had been able to do.

When this had been said, the new chief had to step forward and kneel before the retiring one, who made a cross over his head with his staff three times, and then extended the staff for him to kiss. After this the new chief took the staff in his hand and stood up, and the two changed places. Then the retiring chief knelt before the new one, who offered him the staff to kiss and then made three crosses with it over his head. The retiring chief now stood up and gave the new one his hand, touched his cheeks with his own, and stepped back, right out of the ceremony altogether.

The new chief now recited his verses. He said that he was a weak and erring mortal for so great an office. He promised to use his authority only for the people's good and to be just without respect of persons.

When this had been said, further ceremonies began.

20

This time, however, the ceremony did not follow the course it had followed for hundreds of years. A foreign power, whose only contact with these people was the purely external one of political domination, had presumed to alter their custom and practice to suit itself.

When the captain had had his say, the crowd showed the first signs of excitement. All eyes were turned to the door of the schoolroom on the balcony. The door remained shut. The retiring chief did not emerge with the staff in his hand.

The master of ceremonies had no set verses for this contingency; such behavior on the part of a retiring chief was without precedent.

Three captains now went without ceremony quickly and resolutely up the steps. They knocked loudly on the door and called to Amalio to come out, as they had something to say to him.

Amalio knew that the door was no protection, so he opened it and came out. The captains told him in plain terms without rhyme that they had come to install the new chief and they earnestly begged him to hand over the staff as custom and his duty commanded.

Amalio would probably have been glad to do so and to go home in peace. But his honor did not permit him to give way now that the men threatened him to his face; for the whole nation would say that he had given way from sheer panic when he saw that things looked ugly and that no soldiers were in sight.

He had no alternative but to declare that the governor had made a decree and that according to this decree he was to remain in office another year, whether the nation liked it or not. He added that he obeyed the governor and not the nation and that he would do as the governor said.

To this the men replied that they gave him two hours for reflection, expecting that he would before that time comply with the customs of the nation, to which he owed his existence and the honor of having been chosen as its chief for the past year. There was no need, they said, to consider at the moment what the government would do to him or to them for disobeying the decree: they would deal with that when it arose. "And at this moment all you have to do is what the nation expects of you, and that is to resign your office to the newly elected jefe, Natividad. In these two hours you can think over, all that may and assuredly will happen if you betray the nation. After two hours it will be too late. Then we shall act—and you know it. It is enough already that you have spoiled the festivities. That alone will never be forgotten, though it will be regarded only as an error on your part."

Without waiting for an answer the men descended the steps and rejoined their companions who were sitting close to the foot of them.

No one came from the crowd inquisitive to hear what Amalio had said. Even among the men involved the interview was not mentioned. They smoked, laughed, and talked. There was music, and the children romped about.

21
An hour might have passed before Amalio came down the steps. The group at the foot of them stayed where they were,

squatting on the ground. They only looked up, expecting that Amalio had come to announce his decision.

Amalio paused at the foot of the steps. He had the staff of office in his hand. He asked whether they had any objection to his going to speak to the secretario.

The head captain replied that he might go where he pleased; he was free to talk to whom he chose and to say what he chose; they took no interest in him whatever before the lapse of the two hours. It was his own affair what he did during that time and his own affair from whom he asked advice. But they would not allow him to leave the square without having given up the staff of office. If he liked he might give it up then and there without any ceremony. But he had to give it up before he left the square.

Amalio went to the north side of the cabildo and knocked at the door of the office, calling out at the same time that it was Amalio and that he wanted to speak to the secretario. Don Abelardo opened the door just wide enough for Amalio to squeeze through.

"Señor Secretario," he said, "I don't know what to do. It looks very bad. Don't you think I had better give way?"

The secretary, who ever since they had let his son go unmolested to the prairie for the horses, knew that his own skin was safe and that if anyone was to be sacrificed it was Amalio, said, "Don Amalio, you cannot do that. You cannot give way to these rebels. You are presidente here. You are an official and must stick to your post. As an official you have to obey the decree of the governor. If you do not, you will be shot for disobeying the orders of the government. I have just got through to Jovel. The soldiers, a squadron of cavalry with three machine guns, are already on their way. You need not be afraid. The whole might of the Mexican government stands behind you."

To talk of the whole might of the Mexican government sounded very fine. It was as poetic and soul-shattering as the phrase "The people are marching against the enemy." But it only has that ring when it sweeps in heavy type across the front pages of the special editions. At the sight of it the most hard-boiled of anti's fall flat on their backs—which, however, have been so well padded by opportunism and compromise that an unexpected fall cannot break them.

Upon Amalio, this fine flourish of the whole might made no impression whatever. The whole might he knew was no bigger than a battalion. He knew the distance from the garrison and he knew his own people. Unless this whole might was in the plaza within ten minutes it made no difference to him whether it consisted of six men and a sergeant or of half a million disciplined troops.

He hesitated for a moment and thought of asking whether he might stay in the office with the secretary. But the secretary had long since made up his mind that such a guest would be dangerous. When blows are flying about, one of them may easily go astray; and there might not be time to make sure that the secretary was not struck by accident.

So he left the Indian no time to request hospitality. "The best thing you can do, don Amalio," he said hurriedly, "is to go up again now to the schoolroom. Here you are in my office without your delegates. That might easily arouse the suspicion that we were hatching some plot against your nation. That would do you no good, and I might be accused of underhand methods and improper interference. Just go up quietly to the schoolroom. Nothing can happen to you. You are under the protection of the governor."

The Indian went to the door without saying a word. Don Abelardo again opened it just wide enough for Amalio to squeeze through, and as soon as the last of him was outside the secretary hurriedly shut the door again and bolted it fast.

It did not trouble him that he had lied to the Indian. He had not yet got through to Jovel and so no soldiers were on the march, in order with the help of machine guns to make law of the governor's cupidity.

The ancient customs of the Mexican nation lay far outside the governor's range of vision; and so he thought that a decree of his could change a people's custom overnight.

Amalio went up the steps again, unhindered and unquestioned. Nobody seemed to notice him. The group at the foot of the steps paid no attention at all. They went on talking together and some young fellows struck up a tune on mouth organ and guitar.

The crowd on the plaza seemed to become more cheerful. Here and there they began their customary dances.

22

And then suddenly silence fell. Every sign of merrymaking ceased.

Many of the groups busily packed up. The children were summoned and kept close at hand by their fathers and mothers. The babies were wrapped up and tied to the women's backs. The men took up their packs.

Yet all sat down again. And now every eye was fixed on the cabildo.

The group which had escorted the newly elected chief retreated about twenty paces. Then the three captains advanced to the foot of the steps. From there the senior captain shouted up loudly, "Amalio, the two hours are up. We have come to receive the staff of office in order to hand it over to the new chief. Natividad has been lawfully elected by the grown men of our barrio according to our custom. Your time is up. Hand over the staff."

Amalio had come out of the schoolroom and was standing at the balcony railing. When the captain had done he said, "By the governor's decree I am not to give up the staff but to keep it for another year."

Neither the captains nor anyone else of the troop made any answer. Yet, as though the whole crowd on the plaza had heard every word Amalio said, all those thousands rose to their feet.

It would have relieved the suffocating suspense if they had shouted or cheered. But they were silent. There was only the whimpering of a child here and there; and a few dogs barked from excitement and fright when the whole crowd rose.

And now from far behind, from the far edge of the crowd where there was a group clinging to it like froth on the tip of a spreading wave—not the ceremonial groups at all—some young men sprang forward.

They ran in a close pack, and so it was impossible to count how many there were. There might have been six or there might have been ten.

Half like fleeing deer, half like charging tigers, they rushed precipitately around the edge of the crowd to the cabildo. It was hardly running—they sprang forward in long leaping strides, their bodies almost parallel with the ground. Each had a machete in his hand, and as he ran he held it outstretched in front of him.

They were barefoot, and their legs too were naked. Shirt-like blouses, much mended but spotlessly washed, were caught up and knotted between their legs, and swelled out in the wind as they flew along.

They clung so closely together as they ran that no one in the crowd could recognize their faces. Their movements, too, were so rapid and spasmodic that their faces were distorted. Their mouths gaped wide and their eyes were compressed to tiny slits. Their foreheads were furrowed deeply by their excitement and their long black hair floated about their heads. All this so disguised them that little was to be seen of their usual appearance.

It took them no more than a few seconds to cover the distance between the far edge of the crowd and the steps. They took the steps in two strides and then they were on the balcony.

Amalio, who could see the whole crowd and its farthest groups from the balcony, had seen these men leap forward and he knew at once what it meant. He flew into the schoolroom, shouted a hurried word to his wife and children, and shut and barred the door.

The door had a padlock on the outside only. From inside it could only be shut by a wooden bar, which had been set in for the convenience of the travelers who spent the night there. Two of the men put their shoulders to the door and it flew from its hardwood hinges.

A piercing cry tore into the silence that rested on the waiting crowd below. It came from Amalio's wife and it was the only sound that reached the square. The group around the new chief, who were closest to the cabildo, heard also a brief scuffle and the dull thud of falling bodies.

For the merest fraction of a second one of the men appeared on the balcony and called out "Ahoa!" as he tossed the staff so adroitly to the head captain that it was caught without having touched ground.

The group around the new chief took this as a good omen; for it is considered an insult to the staff of office if it is ever let rest on the ground. The chief's staff, which is to an Indian what the king's scepter is in other lands, has always to be in the hand of the chief; and when the chief is working or sleeping his staff has either to be laid on the little altar in his house before the image of the saint or else be tied to the cross—which is always to be found in the hut of a chief—with his headcloth or the woolen sash he wears around his loins by day.

And now there came flying out of the schoolroom and over the balcony railing onto the grass below first Amalio's head and then the heads of his wife and children. Immediately after the heads came the bodies, hacked to pieces.

All this happened so quickly that it must have seemed to all those whose eyes were fixed on the cabildo like a frenzied dream. Ten seconds at most had passed from the moment when the men reached the foot of the steps to the moment when the last human fragment was tossed in a wide arc over the railing.

And now the men came out—though it was hardly a coming out, for they took the balcony railing as one man in one leap, staggered for a step or two after alighting and then, recovering themselves, sprang along the edge of the crowd with a swinging stride; and before any eye could hold them they had vanished into the bush on the far side of the square.

Any man who for any reason had not so far stood up, stood up now—the women too. Some held their children aloft.

All eyes were turned toward the new chief. The captains lifted him shoulder high so that every member of their nation should see him.

In his right hand he held aloft the staff of office with its silver knob and the black silk tassel bound around it below the knob. The black silk tassel was the sign that the staff belonged not to a small pueblo or to a small tribe but to a great nation made up of several tribes and barrios.

As Natividad waved the staff in greeting to all the people of the nation, one single shout of triumph was raised by all these thousands of Indians—men, women, and children.

23

The crowd, knowing well what was going to happen, had already packed up to go. The cry of triumph was their parting act as one united people. The sound of it—the only national anthem they knew and could sing—still hung in the air as the huge gathering began to break up. It was now composed once more of tribes, families, groups, and individuals. Each had his own way to go, one a stiff climb into the mountains, another a level path over the prairie; and each took his own course and went at his own pace so as to get along unhindered and as he pleased.

The crowd broke up and fell apart so rapidly that in less than half an hour after that exultant shout the whole wide plaza was as empty as though a wind had swept every object and every morsel of humanity before it.

Not even a scrap of paper remained to show that here on the great plaza thousands had been encamped since dawn for no other purpose than to testify to their existence and to make known that, so long as they existed, they meant to defend what their forefathers had taught them to regard as customary and right.

10

 While all this was going on outside, the secretary, his wife, and his children were prostrate before the image of the Virgin on the altar in their living room, nervously saying the beads of their rosaries, which they piously held in hands damp with fear, imploring the Holy Virgin to protect them from the rage of the savages. They vowed to commemorate her help by a pilgrimage to Tila, to present her with twenty pesos in cash and twelve one-peso candles. The Holy Virgin took on her pious worshipers and carried out her part of the bargain by removing the Indians quietly and with speed, as soon as they were satisfied that the staff of office had passed into the right hands.

It had never been their intention to call the secretary to account. He was not a member of their nation and therefore he was not bound by their customs and traditions. Their plan had been to leave the square as soon as their aim had been achieved, and they followed their plan without considering whether don Abelardo was saying his beads or not. Their national assembly had nothing to do with the good graces of the Virgin Mary.

All the same, don Abelardo and his wife were convinced that it was due only to the Mother of God and their pious prayers and vows that the Indians had not troubled themselves about the secretario but behaved as though he did not exist.

Don Abelardo and his wife did not, of course, make the promised pilgrimage to Tila, as they could hardly have been expected to do, since it was a pilgrimage which brought many discomforts and even more expenses in its train. Nor did they offer up the promised twenty pesos, and this too is quite understandable, since a few days later a Syrian dealer came through the place with so many beautiful dresses to show that the secretary's wife said she must either have one of them or die. And to buy it, those twenty pesos were necessary. Indeed, the image of the Virgin in the secretary's living room had to be content with the cheapest oil, on which a further saving was made because the secretary's wife used the thinnest wicks which swam in the oil in a metal dish and cost ten centavos a dozen.

2

The secretary had succeeded in telephoning Jovel at about midday. But it was impossible to get to the commandant of the garrison personally, for it was New Year's Day and it is well known that a New Year's Eve precedes every New Year's Day. The commandant had taken such a heavy part in this that it was five o'clock in the evening of the next day before he could ask his adjutant whether anything had occurred since he was last on the scene.

Since the wires as usual were trailing over the ground the message reached the orderly room in a series of incoherent jerks. The secretary could not get into direct communication with the garrison. His message had to be telephoned on from one place to another. Each relay extended the message verbally and embroidered it according to the temperament and powers of hearing of the receiver.

Hence the message when it reached the garrison was that fifty thousand Indians of Pebvil were in open rebellion and had murdered their chief and the secretary and the entire families of both.

Only the guard was present in the garrison. The soldiers had been allowed out because of the New Year festival, and did not come back until ten o'clock at night, when a good many of them were half gone.

The commandant had other plans for New Year's evening; and besides he did not want to arouse the peaceful town from its holiday sleep for no reason. It would have meant calling out the soldiers who were stowed away in every corner and cranny of the town, celebrating the beginning of a new year.

His noncommittal attitude was confirmed when further inquiries late in the afternoon elicited that the Indians had all moved off and that only their chief had been murdered and that their secretary, a Mexican, was alive and had telephoned himself.

So the commandant ordered a captain to ride next morning to Pebvil with thirty men to find out on the spot what had really happened and whether there was any need to send a larger body to occupy the place for an extended period.

3

It was on the morning of the day after that don Gabriel arrived at Pebvil. He was combing the independent Indian villages for laborers for the monterías.

Don Abelardo told him the whole story just as his terrors dictated it.

Don Gabriel, for purposes of business, took great trouble to read the character of people from their expression and behavior. He tried now to apply the rudiments of this science. It was, however, rather a case of testing his science by what he knew already, for he knew don Abelardo well enough to know how to handle him for business purposes.

As soon as don Abelardo had poured out his tale, he said, "I must say, don Abelardo, I am struck with admiration of the un-exampled personal courage you showed in the face of thousands of rebel Indians. I don't suppose the whole of Mexican history has another such example of cool-headedness and bravery in face of thousands of murderous savages. It was wonderful how you stepped out alone into the open without a revolver and told this excited mob to go quietly to their homes, at the very moment when the hands of those savages were still dripping with the blood of murdered men. I know I never could have done it. I would have crept into the darkest corner with my wife and done nothing but kneel before the Purísima."

"To tell the truth, don Gabriel," don Abelardo answered modestly, "I did shudder for a few moments when the pieces flew out over the veranda."

"Obviously, you must have been a little upset," said don Gabriel adroitly. "It is a sign of the real hero to know the dan-ger he is in. And to tremble on occasion is the undisputed right of every hero; for if a man does not tremble, he does not know danger; and if he cannot estimate danger properly, he can never be called a hero when danger stares him in the face."

"You're right, don Gabriel," said the secretary. "That's ex-actly how it was with me. But I put compulsion on myself and just showed those fellows what a Mexican is capable of. I up-held my authority. The people saw at once that there was no playing the fool with me. That is why they did not hesitate to obey the command to go quietly to their homes."

"I will take very good care," said don Gabriel as though he were already in the presence of the governor, "that your gal-lant deed is known far and wide. Leave it to me. I know the governor and the jefe políticos, and your magnificent conduct shall be made known in the right quarters. Such an exploit must not be forgotten. It must shine abroad as a radiant example of official gallantry in an isolated post. As soon as I get to Tuxtla I will tell all the correspondents of the periódicos to have it published. Once it's in the newspapers your conduct will never be forgotten. Newspapers live, though men must perish one after the other. I know all the correspondents and they will all be glad to do me a good turn."

Don Gabriel was not such a fool as to believe the story the secretary had dished up for him. He had been a secretary himself. He knew better than anybody how a man behaved on such an occasion. The archbishop of Mexico himself could not have persuaded don Gabriel that any secretary, whatever he looked like, whatever his name, however many revolvers he had in his belt, whatever his gift of gab, would ever really behave as don Abelardo had said that he had behaved. Don Gabriel knew himself and he knew some dozens of secretaries, and he would have bet a hundred to one that neither he nor any one of those dozens would have proved an exception to the rule.

Knowing himself, he knew don Abelardo well enough too. And he had sized him up correctly. After this talk he could have got anything out of him he asked—his wife, his best horse, and a hundred Indians for the monterías, if don Abelardo had had the disposal of them.

Don Gabriel was not there to listen to his bragging nor to praise him far above the unknown soldier nor to make him covert promises of the presidency of the Republic. He was there to buy up Indians for the monterías and all he said and did was in the pursuit of this high aim.

He did not so far see very clearly how the Indians were to be got into his outspread net, but he already had some plans. He was only waiting for the arrival of the soldiers in order to get to work. He hoped that the major or the colonel in command would be open to a deal. Even colonels are men, and therefore have an eternal need of money and very little care for the fate of other men except as solutions to their own financial difficulties. When it is a case of Indians who have little claim even to be treated as men at all, there is no moral reason to suppose they have fates to care about.

4

Don Gabriel and don Abelardo were about to sit down to their lunch when a troop of cavalry under the command of a captain rode up to the cabildo. They had taken their time. The captain had halted in order to make a little expedition to a neighboring rancho, because the ranchero's pretty niece was just then on a visit there.

The captain had the intelligence common to officers, and it told him that the Indians could wait; they would still be there two days later, for they have their land and do not run away. It was by no means so certain that he would find the niece there next day, for she lived at Tapachula and might have had to return there.

The captain was not only intelligent; he was also knowing in the ways of the world, which has no direct connection with the conduct of war or the drilling of soldiers. He got active-service allowances for this dangerous expedition. Other countries frequently go to war merely for the opportunity of paying their officers war bonuses. Mexico enjoys this privilege only in a limited degree. For this reason generals and other ranks have to look to military revolutions and Indian rebellions to put them on active-service pay. If officers could not have active-service pay now and then, or at least be kept in constant expectation of it with the help of scare-mongering articles in the papers, they would soon turn sour and even take to politics.

So one must not blame the captain if he thought of his own advantage and tried to spin the expedition out. Even quarters of a day would be paid as whole days. If Pebvil had not had a telephone, which for all he knew might be working, the captain would no doubt have made a long detour before arriving at his destination. And he would have accounted for the delay by saying that he had had to give battle to the Indians more than once before he could enter the place.

It is not so rare an occurrence as people in Greenland may suppose to give battle to rebellious Indians and hordes of bandits in the course of which numerous machine guns and their ammunition fall into the hands of the Indians or the bandits, since the fortunes of war cannot be foreseen. The day after the battle the leader of the bandits comes along and pays the general a handsome sum for the captured machine guns. The leader of the bandits or the chief of the rebellious Indians knows the value of a machine gun—and if not, the general lets him know a few days beforehand how much he will have to pay for the machine guns which he will capture in the battle.

These little deals are mere bagatelles. To talk of betraying the country and squandering the property of the State is all very relative. On the battlefields of Europe, where, according to the belief of excitable citizens, the honor and existence of their country are at stake, the deals are of far vaster dimensions. That is the only difference. And it is only by a regrettable accident that these worthy citizens ever find out that their industrial magnates sell oil, coal, submarines, artillery, warships, and armor plate to foreign powers twice as cheaply as to their own beloved fatherland. The conduct of a Mexican general makes such a poor appearance only because it is pursued in the open and because it is concerned with sums which the citizen can comprehend. It is only when these deals start at hundreds of millions that there is the possibility, in fact the certainty, of public policy's forbidding an inquiry. For as soon as public policy comes in, publicity goes out; and since all concerned, including the judge of the highest court, have their snouts in the same trough, there will be no telling tales out of school.

One must not forget in this connection that in the case of all deals which start at a hundred million dollars, pounds, or marks, only those people have the right to a share who also have the right to the ear of the government.

5

The captain of this little expedition would think himself lucky to make a hundred pesos at the outside. If a general had been in command don Gabriel would probably not have been able to make any profit out of this Indian election.

The captain gave the order to dismount and had the sergeant take over. Don Abelardo and don Gabriel came up and welcomed the officer. The gentlemen shook each other heartily by the hand. While they did so each was already thinking how much he could hope to make in some way or another from or by the others.

An Indian servant girl brought a gourd of water and the captain washed off the dust. Then he accepted don Abelardo's invitation to share the meal which had just been placed on the table.

This suited don Gabriel's book because business goes much more smoothly at table, particularly when it is a good table, than in more uninviting circumstances.

The caballeros did, in fact, come straight to the point without losing any time on profitless talk.

"The place seems utterly dead," said the captain.

"That's true, Captain," replied don Abelardo. "The men have all cleared out. Only the women and children are here."

"Do you know who it was that killed the jefe and his family?" asked the officer.

"No, I don't," said don Abelardo. "From the door I could see the murderers approaching, but they ran so quickly and so close to one another that I could not recognize one of them. They were wearing no hats, and as their hats are the only mark by which you can tell their tribes, I can't even say where the men came from. My conviction is that the murderers do not belong to this nation here but were called in from outside to carry out the sentence. The leading men of the nation did this deliberately to remove all suspicion and to make it impossible for a punitive expedition to be lawfully sent against the nation. And we can do nothing against them unlawfully. If we called the nation to account without knowing whether the murderers belonged to the nation or had been called in by it, we would be guilty of an unlawful act which neither you nor the señor Gobernador could answer for to the government."

"Then I don't know what there is for me to do here," said the officer. "My instructions were to restore law and order. But there is not a soul to be seen. And the new jefe is innocent in the eyes of the law, for we cannot prove that he hired the assassins. There are no means of coming by the proof of it. On the contrary, we must recognize the new jefe as the properly elected chief of the nation whether we like it or not. If we reject him, the people will elect him again and again."

"That is all very true, mi Capitán," said the secretary. "Yet we cannot leave things as they are, since a disturbance of the peace has taken place. As a matter of authority you must do something to show the nation that they cannot do as they like, and that decrees and regulations of the government must be obeyed."

"Bueno," the captain agreed. "Muy bien, muy bien. Pero, pero—that's all very well, but what do you think I can do?"

"I don't exactly know myself," replied the secretary. "If there were only a few men about the place we could round them up and shoot them as a warning. It always has a good effect and shows the nation that we govern it and have the power to carry out the orders of the government."

"I am in a very difficult position," said the officer. "I have to send in a report to the jefe de las operaciones militares, and I must do something here. I cannot simply go away and report that I found the place in a peaceful condition and did nothing but keep my men here a few days and then march them back again. It might bring me a severe reprimand. I wish you could tell me what I'm to do. You know these people and you know how to impress them with the powers of the government. To pack up without doing a thing would make me look ridiculous. And the Indios would think they were the masters here. We can't allow that."

Don Gabriel now joined in. "Perhaps you might wait a day or two, Captain. Sometimes something turns up of itself if you give it time."

"That's a good idea," said the captain. "We'll wait and see what turns up in the course of today or tomorrow."

Then the captain telephoned the garrison to report and ask for further instructions. When his call finally got through he was told that the general's orders were that he do as he thought best and come back as soon as he was sure that such events were not likely to occur again. In this way the whole responsibility was put upon the captain's youthful shoulders and the general was not implicated.

6

The caballeros now passed the time playing cards and drinking. At about four o'clock in the afternoon an opportunity came along that helped each one of them out of the difficulties in which he found himself.

Fourteen Indians belonging to the nation came across the square on their way home to their barrio, which lay to the east.

They had been in Balún-Canán to the Christmas market to sell hides, young pigs, and petates and to buy in exchange articles of domestic or agricultural use.

They were entirely innocent of all that had gone on New Year's Day; they had been elsewhere. They did not even know anything about it, otherwise they would certainly not have crossed the square in full view. It was equally obvious that they had met no one on the road who could have given them a word of warning to avoid the central village. They had come over the mountains as it was the shortest way to the cabildo. If they had come any other way they would have been able to see the soldiers' camp in time.

The presence of soldiers is always suspicious everywhere on earth. Whether a man is a civilized European or a half-civilized Indian he instinctively keeps out of soldiers' way.

In this case, however, the Indians had no sooner emerged from their mountain path than they were already so close to the outposts they could not turn back. To do so would have aroused the suspicion of the sentry, who would have opened fire on them without hesitation. And as the soldiers had horses every man of them would soon have been captured.

For these reasons the men continued quietly on their way. The soldiers, seeing them passing quietly along to the cabildo, did not arrest them and take them before the officer in command.

The men had chosen the way through the central village not only because it was the shortest to their barrio but also because most of them had to see the secretary. One had letters, another had a message from a merchant, another had been commissioned by the secretary to buy a few things for him in Balún-Canán. And most of them wanted to take the opportunity, now that they had money from the sale of their produce in Balún-Canán, of making payments that were due.

7

The caballeros had put a table out in the portico and it was here they sat playing cards, with the bottle of comiteco within easy reach on a stool.

The Indians came up. They put down their heavy loads and stepped close up to the pillars of the portico, where they stood politely waiting until the secretary saw fit to speak to them and ask them what they wanted.

They greeted both him and the other two caballeros by laying the palms of their hands on their heads and then with a bow stretching out the flat of the hand as a greeting to each in turn.

"Con su permiso, caballeros." The secretary excused himself to his two companions as he got up and went to the men.

He asked them to come into the office and discharge their commissions. The Indians handed over the letters and the articles they had been asked to buy and those from whom money was due paid the secretary what they owed.

Meanwhile don Gabriel and the officer were left alone in the portico. They stretched and yawned and looked over the square and poured themselves another comiteco and lit one more cigarette. They got lazily to their feet and stamped about to bring the life into their legs and sat down again.

8

"If you'll listen to me, Captain," don Gabriel then began, "this is the very opportunity you were waiting for. It's an opportunity that won't come your way a second time. If you go among the barrios with your troops you will not catch sight of a single man. The news that you were visiting each barrio in turn in order to pick out a few men to bring before the courts would spread like a cannon shot. The best thing you can do, and the only thing, is to arrest these fellows here and take them back with you as prisoners. You can leave it to the general or the court what they do with the prisoners. Anyway, you will not have gone on your mission of pacification to no purpose."

"Maravilloso," the captain cried. "That is a capital idea of yours, don Gabriel. You could not have had a better. You are right. I'll leave it to the general what he does with them. And whatever he does it won't worry me. I can see you were a good secretary. You know how these matters should be handled."

The captain summoned the sergeant and ordered him to take the men prisoners as soon as they had completed their business with the secretary.

The fourteen Indians were put in the prison, where there was just enough room for four at a squeeze.

9

The day came to an end and the caballeros were seated at supper.

When the Indian girl had cleared the table don Gabriel said, "There is another thing you might do with the prisoners, Captain."

Don Gabriel had already discussed it with don Abelardo before supper, when the captain was parading his men and detailing sentries for the night, and made sure of his support on the quiet.

"What could I do with the prisoners, don Gabriel?" asked the captain.

"There might be objections to taking them with you," don Gabriel explained. "They might run away. This whole Indian nation might fall upon your troops and set them free and neither you nor one of your men would survive."

"There is something to that," the officer replied reflectively.

"And what will they do with the fellows at Jovel? Nothing at all," don Gabriel replied to his own question. "They'll set them free as soon as they prove that they were not here during the rebellion. They will be able to prove they were in Balún-Canán. So what is the good of all this bother with them? My advice is to sentence them here on the spot yourself."

"But I've no right to shoot them," the captain objected.

"That's just it," said don Gabriel. "It's just because you have no right to shoot them that you can do something else which will be just as effective. Sentence the prisoners to a heavy fine. As they belong to this nation which has either committed the murder, or caused it to be committed, the nation will take the fine on itself. That will mean that every man will have to pay his share and they will learn that they cannot play with the government."

"That's true," said the officer. "What do you say, don Abelardo? You are the secretary here and it is for you to say."

"In my opinion," replied the secretary, "don Gabriel's suggestion is the best we could hit on. A fine will bring it home to these people better than shooting or imprisonment. They care nothing about either. It has no effect. I know that from experience. I've been secretary here long enough to know how to put the fear of the government into them."

"If that's your opinion, don Abelardo," said the captain, "then I can make a start. My orders are to consult with you over the proper punitive measures and the means of preventing further rebellions and to carry out your proposals insofar as they concern my mission."

"Good!" don Gabriel now said. "Then we are agreed in principle and can now proceed to details. I suggest that a fine of one hundred and fifty pesos shall be paid for each prisoner. But we all have to live. You too, Captain. Let's say that you take fifty pesos a head, which we'll say nothing about. That will remain between ourselves, caballeros. Don Abelardo and I take fifty pesos a head to your chief, the general. We'll make out the receipts here at fifty pesos. The general will never ask the people any questions. He does not want to be bothered with interrogating Indians who cannot speak Spanish. Besides, we'll put the fellows right out of the way, too far for anyone to interrogate them."

"How do you mean, out of the way?" asked the officer.

"I'll simply take them along to the monterías where they can work off their fines. Before they come back from there the garrison at Jovel will have changed its commanding officer a dozen times."

Don Gabriel had put all this in so clear a light that the captain soon saw it was the best possible outcome of his punitive expedition.

10

The officer was no scoundrel—it was simply his eternal poverty, the curse of his existence. Money was just as welcome to him as to any other man whose expenses exceed his income.

Being a really good and efficient officer, he knew the characteristics of his superior officers by heart. A proper knowledge and appreciation of his superiors is of more use to a subordinate in skipping a grade or two and rising to important positions in the army than any other branch of knowledge, not excluding a comprehensive knowledge of military science. A proper knowledge of his superior officers is a hundred times more necessary to the speedy promotion of an officer than gallantry in face of the enemy or the capture singlehanded of an armed fort. Officers who have a fine feeling regarding their generals have no opportunity of capturing forts or strongholds: they do not get near enough to the enemy for that. Their special branch of knowledge makes them more important in back areas. And as war is a business like another, there is no secret here and nothing that can be called unworthy of an officer, all the less as all armies in the world have the same view of the attributes which make a man an invaluable officer.

Knowing his general so well the captain naturally knew his necessities. And to lighten these necessities was his duty as a subordinate. Fourteen times fifty pesos in hard cash would be very much more welcome to the general than fourteen lousy Indians brought along as prisoners.

The captain had no doubt whatever that he would be highly commended for having brought the punitive expedition to so effective and tactful a close.

The treasury was naturally not forgotten in this financial

deal. Fines for disturbances of the peace were a common occurrence. In the annual budget of the State there was the following entry:

"Fourteen Indians of the Pebvil district fined for disturbance of the peace, each, pesos—1.50."

The public, and in particular the reporters of the big American newspapers, could not say that the poor Indians in Mexico were harshly punished when they were only fined a peso and a half for so grave an offense as disturbance of the peace. A government which punished rebellious Indians so mildly deserved to be called highly civilized and upright, since it had such an understanding sympathy for the poor Indian brother.

The captain, who had been so handsomely remembered in the division of the spoil, did not trouble to remember that the accounts were hardly accurate.

This inaccuracy was a trivial one. It was no more than that the nation was given no opportunity of taking the fine of the fourteen innocent men on its shoulders. For whether the nation did so or not made no difference to the fate of the fourteen prisoners, who in any case would have been taken off to the monterías by don Gabriel, so that they could work off their fines and the agent's commission.

11

The prisoners were brought out next day. The captain gave them to understand, with the help of don Gabriel and don Abelardo as interpreters, that they had been sentenced to fines of a hundred and fifty pesos each for the murder of their jefe and his family and that, as they didn't have the money, they were to go to the monterías as indentured laborers with don Gabriel. They were warned that if they attempted to escape not only they but their sons and fathers would be shot.

After they had had the terms of the contract explained to them they were allowed to go to their barrios to say good-by to their families; meanwhile they were to be in readiness to start for the monterías on the appointed day.

They considered themselves extremely lucky to have got so cheaply out of a rebellion with which they had nothing to do. And they expressed their thanks with bows to the captain, to don Gabriel, and don Abelardo.

The captain retired the same day with his troops. It took him three days to reach the garrison because he spent two days at the ranch where the ranchero had the pretty niece staying with him.

The general promised to see that he got his majority in two months' time. And he kept his word.

Don Gabriel made the fourteen Indians who had come his way produce sureties, and the contracts were witnessed by the secretary. This done, he set off on a round of fincas to buy up indebted peons from the finqueros who wanted money.

In all this don Gabriel was entirely innocent. It was the fault of the monterías, which devoured Indians by the hundreds, in order that citizens and their wives in the United States and Europe could have mahogany furniture and the bankers and industrial lords mahogany writing tables.

Mahogany, when landed at New York, sold for seventy to a hundred and twenty dollars a ton, depending on the market. At such a price it was impossible to take the so-called rights of Indians literally, or any of those phrases about comradeship and respect for humanity. In the proper conduct of any business that is to show a profit there is no time for dealing with phrases and ideas of world betterment. That is left to idealists, who are paid to introduce such phrases into films as sob stuff which will fill the house.

A man who has power and makes no use of it is a fool. Nobody gives anything away, and if your business fails your creditors give you no quarter. The only thing is to keep your nerve. Grab where and when there is anything to be grabbed.

For poetic justice you must look to opera, and to the Easter Service when sermons are preached about the Resurrection of the Savior of mankind. The Church does not go away with empty hands. You cannot make dollars with the cramp of conscience in your throat. It is useless to expect dollars to rain down from the sky. No instances have occurred to justify such a hope. Dollars must be hard-earned. Many hands and brains must be exerted to the utmost before you can get your hundred dollars for a ton of mahogany. And if nobody fells the mahogany in the primeval forests of America and floats it down the forest rivers, there can be no mahogany cupboards and no mahogany cabinets. You cannot have cheap mahogany and at the same time save all those innocent Indians who perish by the thousands in the jungle to get it for you. It must be either one or the other. Either cheap mahogany or respect for the humanity of the Indian. The civilization of the present day cannot run to both, because competition, the idol of our civilization, cannot tolerate it. Pity? Yes—with joyfulness and a Christian heart. But the dollar must not be imperiled.

FOR THIRTY-FIVE YEARS, *from 1876 to 1911, power in Mexico was in the hands of one man, Porfirio Díaz. Mexico's constitution had been altered to give sanction to his re-elections, which were assured by his appointment of state governors and other officials. Opposition was controlled by a ruthless federal police, called the* rurales. *It was a reign of peace and prosperity for the few and dire poverty for the many—half the entire rural population of Mexico was bound to debt slavery. Big landowners and foreign capital were favored as more and more Indians lost their communal lands.*

In the final decade of Díaz's rule, however, opposition strengthened, and before his last engineered re-election he promised a return to democratic forms—which after the election he gave no sign of honoring. In 1910 revolution broke out; independent rebel armies under the leadership of Pancho Villa, Emiliano Zapata, Francisco Madero, and others upset the power of the landlords and eventually overthrew the Díaz regime.

In what have become known as the "Jungle Novels," B. Traven *wrote, during the 1930's, an epic of the birth of the Mexican revolution. The six novels—*Government, The Carreta, The March to Caobaland, The Troza, The Rebellion of the Hanged, *and* The General from the Jungle—*describe the conditions of peonage and debt slavery under which the Indians suffered in Díaz's time. The novels follow the spirit of rebellion that slowly spread through the labor camps and haciendas, culminating in the bloody revolt that ended Porfirio Díaz's rule.*

In the 1920's, when B. Traven arrived in the country, peonage, although officially abolished by the new constitution of 1917, was still a general practice in many parts of Mexico.

230

The author observed the system at first hand in Chiapas, the southernmost province, a mountainous and heavily forested region, where the jungle novels, as well as many other of his stories, are set.